INFANTILE ORIGINS
OF
SEXUAL IDENTITY

INFANTILE ORIGINS
OF
SEXUAL IDENTITY

Herman Roiphe, M.D.,
and
Eleanor Galenson, M.D.

INTERNATIONAL UNIVERSITIES PRESS, INC.

Library of Congress Cataloging in Publication Data

Roiphe, Herman, 1924–
    Infantile origins of sexual identity.

    Bibliography: p.
    Includes index.
    1. Infant psychology. 2. Identity (Psychology)
3. Sex (Psychology) 4. Parent and child.
5. Psychoanalysis. I. Galenson, Eleanor, 1916–
II. Title. (DNLM: 1. Identification (psychology) —
In infancy and childhood. 2. Sex behavior — In
infancy and childhood. WS 105.5.Sr R74li]
BF720.S48R64   155.4'22   81-14290
ISBN 0-8236-2368-8   AACR2

Manufactured in the United States of America

TO OUR CHILDREN

who taught us to be parents and paved the way for our understanding of infants, parents, and their interactions.

CONTENTS

PREFACE

The events of the preoedipal period remained relatively obscure until the direct observational research undertaken by Margaret S. Mahler and her co-workers. While Mahler has consistently emphasized that the separation-individuation process unfolds simultaneously with libidinal-phase progression, emergent aggression, and ego structuralization, her investigations have been focused specifically upon developing object relations. Ours has been the first attempt to correlate the development along each of these axes.

It is the interrelationship existing between instinctual-phase development, self-object differentiation, and other aspects of ego development that has been of particular interest to us. Such interrelationships cannot be clarified, however, until the landmarks of progressive development in these areas have been clearly delineated. This has been the focus of attention in our research. We need to know, for example, that, in relation to drive development, anal-zone awareness is indicated by a certain relatively invariant behavioral sequence, and that yet another behavioral sequence is anal derivative in nature. And similarly for the different aspects of object relations and ego functioning.

Our work has centered upon the later months of the first year and the second year of life, a period of rapid growth and development. We have been particularly interested in elucidating the vicissitudes of libidinal-drive development not only as it was interwoven with other sectors of development in the child but also as it seemed to affect the very fiber of the child-parent relation. In the course of our studies we have become convinced that these early sexual stirrings in the infant stimulate and reactivate corresponding feelings in the parents. We suspect that this is also true with regard to the emergence of aggression, although our data in that area have not yet been analyzed.

As our research proceeded, we became increasingly convinced that we had been engaged in tracing the development of the sense of sexual identity from its vague beginnings during the earliest weeks and months to a definite conscious awareness of specific gender and genital erotic feelings and fantasies by the end of the second year. This definitive awareness has turned out to be a critical factor in ongoing psychological development and has therefore been designated as the beginning of a new psychosexual phase.

One may well ask, as we have so often asked ourselves during the many years of our study, why the army of infant observers and researchers have, with a few notable exceptions, overlooked these astonishingly protean manifestations of early sexuality. Once again, Freud seemed to have understood the problem when he stressed the ubiquity of repression of infantile sexuality. His observation seems to apply not only to adults in general situations but to adults as they relate to their children.

Some parts of this book have already been published in a different form.

Chapters 1 and 2 are based on two articles by Roiphe: "On an Early Genital Phase" (1968) and "Some

Thoughts on Childhood Psychosis, Self and Object"
(1973).

Chapter 4 is taken from "Object Loss and Early
Sexual Development" (1973) by Roiphe and Galenson.

Chapter 5 is based on "A Consideration of the Nature of Thought in Childhood Play" (1971) by Galenson, and "The Choice of Symbols" (1976) by Galenson,
R. Miller, and Roiphe.

Chapter 6 derives from "The Impact of Early Sexual Discovery on Mood, Defensive Organization, and
Symbolization" (1976) by Galenson and Roiphe.

Chapter 7 is taken from "Early Genital Activity
and the Castration Complex" (1972) by Roiphe and
Galenson.

Chapter 9 is based on "Some Observations on the
Transitional Object and Infantile Fetish" (1975) by
Roiphe and Galenson.

Chapter 10 stems from "The Infantile Fetish"
(1973) by Roiphe and Galenson.

Chapter 12 is taken from "Disturbance in Sexual
Identity Beginning at 18 Months of Age" (1973) by Galenson, S. Vogel, S. Blau, and Roiphe.

Chapters 13 and 14 are derived from "Some Suggested Revisions Concerning Early Female Development" (1976), "Development of Sexual Identity" (1979),
and "The Preoedipal Development of the Boy" (1980),
all by Galenson and Roiphe.

We are very grateful to the publishers and editors
for making available to us the material that originally
appeared in their journals and books.

To *The Psychoanalytic Study of the Child* for
"On an Early Genital Phase," 23:348–365. New

York: International Universities Press.
"The Impact of Early Sexual Discovery on Mood, Defensive Organization, and Symbolization," 26: 195–216. New York: Quadrangle Books.
"Some Thoughts on Childhood Psychosis, Self and Object," 28:131–145; "The Infantile Fetish," 28: 147–166. New Haven: Yale University Press.

To the *Psychoanalytic Quarterly* for
"Early Genital Activity and the Castration Complex," 41:334–347.
"Object Loss and Early Sexual Development," 42:73–90.
"Some Observations on the Transitional Object and Infantile Fetish," 44:206–231.

To International Universities Press for
"A Consideration of the Nature of Thought in Childhood Play," in: *Separation-Individuation: Essays in Honor of Margaret S. Mahler*, ed. J. B. McDevitt & C. F. Settlage, pp. 41–59.
"Development of Sexual Identity: Discoveries and Implications," in: *On Sexuality*, ed. T. B. Karasu & C. W. Socarides, pp. 1–17.

To the *International Review of Psycho-Analysis* for
"Disturbance in Sexual Identity Beginning at 18 Months of Age," 2:389–397.

To the *Journal of the American Academy of Child Psychiatry* for
"The Choice of Symbols," 15:83–96.

To the *Journal of the American Psychoanalytic Association* for
"Some Suggested Revisions Concerning Early Female Development," in: *Supplement, J. Amer.*

Psychoanal. Assn., *Female Psychology*, ed. H. P.
Blum. Vol. 24, No. 5, pp. 29–57.
"The Preoedipal Development of the Boy," 28:805–
827. New York: International Universities Press.

We also wish to thank all those who have in some
way contributed to creating this book. We owe a profound debt to our psychoanalytic teachers who provided us with the psychological framework which has
shaped our thinking. In addition, we acknowledge our
special indebtedness to Dr. Phyllis Greenacre and Dr.
Margaret S. Mahler, whose theoretical formulations
and clinical contributions have served as the foundation
upon which our work has rested.

The mainstay of our project was our permanent
staff. Dr. Edward Sperling and Dr. Eva Sperling were
on our senior faculty for several years, along with Dr.
Sarah Vogel and Dr. Robert Miller. The late Dr. Ruth
Rabinowitch was also a devoted faculty member in the
early years of our project. The selection of cases and the
year-long running of the Nursery, with a never-ending
multitude of daily tasks were for several years carried
out most effectively by Mrs. Alice Childs. Her successor,
Mrs. Catherine Shapiro, had her own inimitable and
thoroughly competent style which not only relieved us
of a great many responsibilities but also added much to
the richness of the work and the avoidance of friction
and discord in such a large and varied group of families.
Dr. Jan Drucker, our staff psychologist, in addition to
acting as an observer, aided immeasurably in the work
of categorizing our material. Last but certainly not least
on our permanent staff was Mrs. Helen Vizzini, our sec-

retary and typist, who not only mothered the infants we studied, but also mothered our trainees, our permanent staff, and ourselves.

More than 70 residents, fellows, graduate students, and trainees collaborated with us over the years. We cannot begin to name these helpful assistants, but we are deeply grateful to them.

We are equally grateful to those who assisted us from a distance. Dr. Jack Wilder, Acting Chairman of the Department of Psychiatry at the Albert Einstein College of Medicine, encouraged us with both financial and professional support during a number of critical periods; he was later followed in an equally devoted fashion by Dr. T. Byram Karasu in his position as Acting Chairman of the Department. Geographically more distant but never personally or professionally so was Dr. Justin D. Call, Chairman of Child and Adolescent Psychiatry at the University of California at Irvine Medical Center, who was an early supporter of our work and gave us much-needed encouragement to proceed with it. Dr. Robert Stoller of Los Angeles played a similar role, sharing with us his enormous expertise in the field of early sexuality. Both of these colleagues have probably influenced us more than they have realized.

Mrs. Natalie Altman, our editor, far exceeded even our optimistic expectations of her share in this enterprise. She has been both merciless and constantly supportive in helping us to organize our material into what we think is a more coherent form. We have faced the task of correlating our infant observational studies with psychoanalytic theory and clinical material derived from adults. This requires a thorough grounding in clas-

sical as well as the more recent psychoanalytic literature. It has been our good fortune that Mrs. Altman's
many years of experience as an editor of psychoanalytic
journals and books uniquely qualified her to perform
this integrative task with us. We can truly say that this
book could not have been written without her.

We also wish to thank Ms. Liza Altman for her ex-
pert editorial assistance and patience as she typed and
retyped the final manuscript.

Without the families who volunteered to be subjects for our research, our study would not have been
possible. To all of them, our heartfelt thanks.

Finally, we owe much to our respective spouses for
their tolerance and their encouragement.

CHAPTER 1

PREOEDIPAL

CASTRATION REACTIONS

One of the most firmly established sets of constructs in psychoanalysis has been that large body of work in which the phallic phase, along with its appropriate dynamic content, is delineated. The most generally accepted theory of the development of sexuality has been that the two sexes develop in much the same way until the onset of the phallic phase at about three years of age. At this time children of both sexes would seem to be little boys (Freud, 1933), with the clitoris substituting for the penis. The child's observation of the anatomical difference between the sexes (Freud, 1925) and the consequent castration complex have a fateful impact on male and female sexual development (Freud, 1931, 1933).

Our clinical experience has led us to reconsider certain aspects of these constructs and to certain extensions in our understanding of genital development. Most spe-

1

cifically, we have found male and female sexual development to diverge considerably earlier than Freud thought. We agree that perception of the genital difference precipitates a castration reaction, but we have found that in both sexes this perception and the reaction to it occur prior to the onset of the oedipal phase. Indeed, we have found that infants, usually between their 15th and 19th months, acquire a distinct awareness of their genitals. This genital awareness occurs with such regularity and exerts such a pervasive effect on all areas of functioning that we have designated it the *early genital phase.* One of the most conspicuous manifestations of the early genital phase is the aforementioned preoedipal castration reaction, a reaction sharply different in boys from what it is in girls: the boys attempt to deny the anatomical difference; the girls acknowledge the difference and become depressed and angry. These differences in reaction have led us to postulate that it is during the early genital phase, during the second half of the second year of life, that the infant begins to take on a discernible sense of sexual identity.

Horney (1924, 1926) and Jones (1927, 1933) questioned Freud's views on feminine sexual development, postulating an early phase of female gender development followed by a secondary phase which was a defensive reaction against the girl's growing awareness of the genital difference. Both Jones (1927) and Melanie Klein (1928) cited evidence of genital sensations in little girls in the second year of life that are associated with oral and anal developments. Their views were complicated, however, by their invocation of an oedipal constellation in the second year, concomitant with this genital arousal. While their conceptual framework of an early oedipal complex is open to serious question, it is not so easy to dismiss the observational underpinnings of a genitality that manifests itself earlier than has generally been supposed and that is involved with preoedipal developmental currents. Horney (1924, 1926), Müller (1932), Payne (1935), and Brierley (1936) all reported on evidence of early (preoedipal) vaginal sensations in girls.

The genital sexual current Freud described is, from the beginning, interwoven with the familiar oedipal triangle. In the boy, the Oedipus complex develops naturally from the phase of his phallic sexuality. The implicit threat of castration results in the repression and abandonment of the Oedipus complex, with the superego established as its heir. In the girl, said Freud, the castration complex precedes and prepares the way for the Oedipus complex. Not until she has passed through the phallic phase, has observed the anatomical difference between the sexes, and has suffered the castration complex and a sense of inferiority and penis envy does the girl enter the oedipal phase, turning from her mother to her father (1931, 1937). It is thus the girl's recognition of the anatomical difference that forces her away from masculinity and masculine masturbation, and toward the development of femininity.

Freud, in 1931 and 1933, concerned himself with the preoedipal development of the girl, emphasizing that the early attachment to the mother did not terminate as early or as decisively as he had thought, but rather continued on into the phallic phase and in some cases was never relinquished.

Brunswick's (1940) paper on the preoedipal phase,

written as the result of discussions of case material with Freud and generally considered to reflect his latest views on the subject, described the girl's preoedipal development as more complicated and longer than had been believed. Brunswick maintained, however, that the discovery of the genital difference did not occur until the third year, and that at first the girl thinks that her lack of a phallus is an individual or accidental occurrence and is therefore remediable. The girl knows about the presence of the clitoris at this time, but not of the vagina. The phallic period is ushered in, according to Brunswick, by the discovery of the genital difference and the resulting greatly heightened infantile sexual activity. Clitoral masturbation becomes intense, and the active libidinal wishes are directed toward the mother. Only when the girl perceives that her mother does not have a penis does she give up hopes of having one herself. She abandons the mother as a love object with far more bitterness than does the boy, and she attempts to transfer her passive strivings to her father in identification with her castrated mother. Her active strivings are sublimated, and find expression in having a child as an adult woman.

Brunswick reminds us that Freud attributed far greater repression of infantile sexuality to the girl than to the boy because the girl's masturbatory acts remind her of the castration trauma. Brunswick added to this the influence of the girl's greater hostility to the mother in connection with the narcissistic hurt of castration, so that the loosening of the girl's attachment to the mother and the inhibition of phallic-phase masturbation are connected.

Discussing observations at variance with established analytic findings concerning the chronology of genital development, Anna Freud (1951, p. 150) reported, "Penis envy, which we expected to see in girls in the phallic phase, appeared with extreme violence according to some of our recordings in girls between 18 and 24 months. In these cases, the responsible factor may have been the bodily intimacy between boys and girls as it exists in a residential nursery where the opportunities for watching other children being bathed, dressed, potted, etc. are countless." Anna Freud tentatively suggested that the provocative force of the observation of the anatomical difference between the sexes produced the extremely violent reactions of penis envy in these children. Such a thesis does not, however, explain the curious age clustering, nor, for that matter, does it explain why there is such a high narcissistic cathexis of the genitals, which is implied in such a reaction.

Lisbeth Sachs (1962) has reported in considerable detail a case of severe castration anxiety in an 18-month-old boy. This youngster had achieved rather solid bowel and bladder control by 18 months. He suddenly refused to use the toilet and would not even enter the bathroom. He became generally tense and panic-stricken and repeatedly expressed the fear that he would lose his penis, that he would be flushed down the toilet, or that he would lose an arm, fingers, or nose. He resisted his mother's efforts to remove his soiled diaper with the expressed fear that his penis would fall off. He also worried that his penis would fall off in the bath and go down the drain. He developed a severe sleep disturbance, awakening from sleep screaming for his mother, although her approach frequently provoked a more intense panic. Apparently he awoke from nightmares of noisily barking dogs, bells, and shooting guns and was frightened by dreams of butterflies touching his body. His fear of noises soon spread to the daytime sounds of screeching brakes, airplanes, the vacuum cleaner, and the washing machine.

This classical description of profound castration anxiety in a young boy would be unremarkable were it not for the unusually early age of its onset. Unfortunately, there is a hiatus in this otherwise rich and detailed clinical study, for it provides no delineation of what factors served to provoke this catastrophic castration reaction. There is, however, some indirect evidence that the little boy had seen his mother exposed. Once, when his mother had scolded him a great deal, he cried, "I don't want my penis. I want to wee-wee from my toushy like mommies do."

Sachs later (1977) reported two additional cases of unmistakable castration reactions developing in boys during the second year of life. In all three of her cases the infant-parent relation was considerably less than optimal. Sachs explained the castration anxiety in these youngsters as arising out of the oedipal conflict during the second year, a far-reaching assertion for which the protocols do not offer firm and satisfactory clinical evidence. In any case, the fact that the three boys developed castration reactions is established beyond reasonable doubt. It should also be noted that the time of onset falls within the age cluster of the cases reported earlier by Anna Freud.

Mahler (1966) alluded to the emergence of preoedipal castration reactions when she wrote: "I must emphasize the importance of the double trauma of toilet training and the discovery (at a much earlier age than we have thought) of the anatomical sexual difference as contributory factors in the genesis of the propensity of girls to depressive moods.... the depressive response—with or without a generally angry mood—has been observed in girls definitely more often than in boys. Their anger toward and disappointment with mother for not having given them a penis could be traced convincingly in several cases" (p. 164).

While working with Margaret Mahler at Masters Children's Center, one of us (Roiphe) had occasion to observe closely a moderately severe castration reaction in a 19-month-old girl, a case similar in many of its details to the one reported by Sachs. The inferences drawn from it, however, were very different.

KATE

Kate was the first-born child of a young couple who had married shortly after they graduated from college. Mrs. D., age 24, had no ambitions for herself other than to be a housewife and mother. Comprehensive psychological tests administered at the Masters Children's Center, although they exposed a degree of conflict and anxiety in the mother, showed no pathological elements. The tests revealed superior and intact intelligence, many ego strengths, and a capacity for warm relationships only somewhat marred by ambivalence. Mrs. D. described her husband as devoted to his family, with high hopes and reasonable prospects in his chosen career as an economist with a large business enterprise. She described Kate as having been a very attractive, alert, good-tempered baby who rarely cried. Kate's development during the first year was unremarkable except for its general precocity and good quality. She sat at four and a half months, crawled at five months, pulled herself to the standing position at six months, began to talk at 10 months, and walked at 11 months.

Kate first came to the Center when she had just turned 13 months. Her energy and vigor were indeed a joy to watch. She alternated between relatively long periods of concentrated and precocious play with toys and a curious exploration of the entire playroom. The contrast between the child and her mother, who sat almost immobile, painfully self-conscious and shy, was striking. Mrs. D. seemed to take an exhibitionistic, almost aggressive pride in her child. In many respects it seemed as if the child almost entirely filled the mother's life during this period. The impression of self-sufficiency Mrs. D. gave, when coupled with her child, was outstanding. From the very beginning of the study the father was away, first in a nearby Army training camp so that Mrs. D. saw him only on weekends, and later overseas.

Kate was 15 months old when her father was sent overseas. She promptly developed a sleep disturbance of moderately severe proportions which lasted for three weeks. It was heralded by difficulty in falling asleep and was soon followed by awakening at night, screaming and thrashing about for 15 minutes or so. Her mother, incapable of comforting her, had the impression that Kate was not entirely awake and did not seem to recognize her. The mother's very approach, touch, and holding seemed in itself unpleasurable and tended to exacerbate the infant's frantic state. Kate's behavior as we observed it in the Center deteriorated markedly. Her almost boundless energy was replaced by what seemed to be extreme fatigue. She began to fall much more frequently than usual and was often irritable and crying, running to her mother for comfort. Most dramatic during this time was the alteration in her social behavior. Her previous approach to adults had been spontaneous and easy and had tended naturally to elicit a response; now the smile and her general facial expression began to take on the character of a grimace. The earlier confident expectation of her ability to win a warm response from others was altered to an almost desperate appeal for attention. Formerly, her every activity exuded a palpable feeling of pleasure and joy in her performance. This now disappeared completely. Whereas Kate had previously been capable of spending relatively long periods exploring or playing with toys without having to hover or return frequently to her mother, now her activity was much more concentrated around the area where the mothers ordinarily sat. Following immediately on her father's departure, she suddenly began to play bye-bye games repetitively, and also evidenced an unusual concentration on the comings and goings of all the people in the nursery group.

Shortly after Kate's father left, she began to manifest a spontaneous awareness of her toilet functions. She first seemed to be aware of bladder urgency, saying "tinkle" on several occasions so that her mother could get her to the potty. Most often, however, her words indicated that she had just wet herself. Somewhat later she also signaled bowel urgency either as she anticipated having a bowel movement or just after having one. For the first time she showed discomfort when she was wet or soiled. Her control gradually improved over the next several months so that she had achieved fairly solid bowel and bladder control by 18 months of age. She was in training pants during the day, had very few bowel or bladder "accidents," and wore diapers only at night.

One day when Kate was 19 months old, she spent the afternoon at the house of one of the little boys from the nursery while her mother was out shopping. The boy had been walking around entirely undressed, and sometime in the late afternoon both children were bathed together. Later that evening at home she mentioned to her mother that the boy had not had any clothes on, and made particular reference to his penis as his "pee-pee maker." She seemed compelled to talk about the afternoon's experience. However, the more she talked about it, the fewer were the direct references to the penis. Ultimately she said that the little boy had "three belly buttons" and a birthmark. (It should be noted that Kate had a somewhat protuberant umbilicus and a birthmark on her hip, neither of which the little boy had.)

From the morning following the exposure experience, Kate, who had achieved fairly solid toilet control, began to have a number of bowel and bladder accidents. Her mother, while troubled by her child's obvious disturbance, reacted relatively mildly to her incontinence. This regression lasted for about 10 days to two weeks, after which she regained control. However, for five or six weeks thereafter she showed what was for her an unusual reaction of mild anxiety to the flush of the toilet. On one occasion when she was urinating and heard an adjoining toilet being flushed, she abruptly interrupted her urination and refused to use the toilet again for the rest of the morning, although she was clearly uncomfortable as a result of her urinary urgency. At another time when she was using the toilet, she pulled a little boy's hair in fury when he made a gesture to flush the toilet.

During this same period Kate became intensely negativistic toward her mother, refusing to comply with even her most rudimentary requests, such as dressing and bathing, whereas before she had been cheerful, easy, and good-tempered. The negativism largely receded as toilet control was re-established. This was followed by some two weeks of a moderate sleep disturbance, which then also subsided.

After the acute negativism receded, her mother reported that Kate seemed contented and self-contained, able to occupy herself at home for long periods of time in wholesome and constructive play. This serenity contrasted with what was observed during the same period in the Center, where Kate was irritable and very frequently broke into tears. The discrepancy in her behavior resulted from the fact that in the nursery setting very frequently one of the children would take away a doll, knock over her blocks, or in some way interfere with Kate's play activity. At this time, in the setting of her acute castration reaction, she was singularly unable to tolerate such interference and would break out into despairing and helpless crying, whereas earlier, when faced with the same type of situation, she had coped with it either by asserting her own interests or shifting to some other activity without any great disturbance.

During the period of Kate's negativism, when her mother found it impossible to get through even the simplest operations, Kate developed a very persistent and widespread speech pattern characterized by such phrases as "something just like I have," "Suzy has a dress just like mine," or, "I have a leg just like Mommy." In connection with the latter statement, it should be noted that one morning on the way to the Center, she became very upset and irritable on seeing a man with one leg amputated. One evening when she saw the flashing light of an airplane in the sky, she said to her mother, "That is a light in the sky just like a star." Although this last instance has the same structure as the others, it differs in that it clearly contains an imaginative leap without the narcissistic anchoring of the other statements. Here Kate has freed herself from the defensive constraint evident in her other remarks and thus achieved a major advance in thinking and linguistic image — the metaphoric form. One day while struggling to put on Kate's sneakers, Mrs. D. said they were just like Barbara's, a somewhat older and much admired child with whom Kate often played. Kate seemed quite intrigued with this idea of similarities rather than differences and readily allowed her mother to put on the sneakers. We think the appeal of the mother's remark rested on its succinct verbalization of Kate's own defensive displacement and denial after seeing the little boy's penis — her resorting to the more comforting thought that he had something just like she had, when she spoke of his three belly buttons and his birthmark.

One day at home Kate was playing with some crayons and deliberately broke a large brown crayon in two, behavior rather unusual for her, since she had shown very little tendency to be destructive with her playthings. After she had broken it she tried to put it together again. When she found that this was impossible she broke into uncontrollable sobbing which lasted for about 45 minutes, notwithstanding her mother's effort to comfort her. The crying subsided only when she had exhausted herself. It seems safe to infer from this fantasy play with the crayon that Kate was making an effort to actively repair the narcissistic injury consequent to the passive confrontation with her castration. The intense sobbing followed when it came home to her that it was impossible to do this and that she could not hope in this way to undo the observation of the anatomic difference between boys and girls. It is also possible that the play signaled a fantasy of a stool-phallus equation (Abraham, 1920, p. 343). In this connection it should be recalled that there had been considerable disturbance in Kate's bowel function earlier in the course of the castration reaction. In any case, there was ample evidence of the fantasy wish to have a penis at this time. Her mother observed that Kate frequently walked about holding some object between her legs.

About two months after having perceived the sexual difference, Kate began to show a striking shift in her response to situations in which other children took something away from her or in some way interfered with her activity. Instead of collapsing in helpless crying, she now began to turn on the other children in furious attack. She might hit the other child, but much more commonly she pulled the child's hair. Her mother was extremely distressed by this aggressive behavior and responded with firm — although not unkind — disapproval. Kate's struggle to internalize her mother's prohibitions against her aggressive outbursts, although often unsuccessful, was touching to watch. When another child took a toy from her, she was heard to say out loud to herself, "Now it is Suzy's turn and soon it will be mine"; or on another occasion, "I shouldn't hurt Jane. I should make nice." Gradually the petting would become rougher, until finally she would grab at Jane's hair and pull.

The hair-pulling may well be related to a sequence of events arising during the period of acute negativism. Kate showed considerable resistance to being bathed and was particularly adamant in her refusal to have her hair washed. Once, in an effort to cajole Kate to permit her hair to be washed, her mother got into the shower with her. Under these circumstances she readily complied. At the time, Mrs. D. was evasive about Kate's response to seeing her mother exposed; only considerably later did we learn that Kate had tried to investigate her mother's genitals. Kate's repeated efforts after this episode to look under the skirts of adult women suggests that she was questioning the existence of a hidden penis.

Kate's reaction to observing the anatomical difference is almost classic in its development as noted in most psychoanalytically oriented infant studies. The noxious experience is sharp and clear-cut and the child's reactions immediate and unambiguous. It is our view, considering the relation of the triad of symptoms — incontinence, negativism, and the sleep disturbance at the time of the earlier separation reaction — that the preoedipal castration reactions, in contrast to the later phallic-oedipal phase castration reactions, not only reflect a threat to the infant's sense of body intactness, but simultaneously are experienced as a threat of object loss.

The stunning effect of the little girl's observation of the boy's penis, reflected in her repetitive recounting of it to her mother without elaboration or distortion, suggests Kate's struggle to establish the reality of the perception. It was only after several hours that organized reactions were mobilized, a process that continued unabated for at least several months. The first organized reaction, unstable as it was, was a defensive displacement and denial of the noxious perception. The penis was no longer alluded to directly as it had been several hours before, but rather she attributed to the little boy a birthmark and three belly buttons. This completed the full circle of denial in that Kate, not the boy, possessed the birthmark and protuberant umbilicus. The denial was pervasive—"I have something just like someone else"—and tended to organize the infant's perceptions, thoughts, and relationships to a remarkable degree. The denial and the almost instant shift to stressing similarities of other parts of the body confirm the observations of Anna Freud and Dorothy Burlingham (1944) of nursery infants. This reaction to the confrontation with the genital difference between the sexes indicates a major undermining of the self representation, particularly of the body self.

But denial was incapable of containing the disruptive, traumatic force of the experience, and within less than 24 hours Kate became incontinent. It is a commonplace of psychoanalytic experience that, in the face of a major disturbance, the acquirements most recently mastered are most subject to loss via regression. We can, however, go beyond this generalization and, on the basis of clinical material, make more specific statements about the dynamic structure of the regressive reaction. Elucidation of the major symptomatic triad in this infant—the incontinence, the coincident negativism, and the sleep disturbance that soon followed—will clarify why we believe that the castration reaction was experienced as a threat of object loss and thereby gained its dynamic disruptive force. This elucidation will require a digression in order to review Kate's responses to her father's departure four months earlier, an event that precipitated a separation reaction of some proportion.

Before her father left, this sturdy youngster was relatively independent of her mother, able to spend long periods in an expansive, joyful, and exhilarated exploration of her physical and human environment. After her father left her range became painfully constricted so that most of her time was spent in a hovering, anxious closeness to her mother. Kate undeniably reacted to the loss of her father, but the major impact of the experience stemmed from the threat it posed of the loss of the more highly invested maternal object. A major developmental thrust at this period in the infant's life is the separation from and casting off of the symbiotic relationship to the mother, in the process of which the infant leans increasingly heavily on the father (see Mahler and Gosliner, 1955; Greenacre, 1966; Abelin, 1971). With the loss of her father, Kate became much more dependent on her mother and was in consequence much more threatened by her maturing independent strivings. We have confirmation for this assertion in the identification with the mother that emerged at this time, a variant on the theme that an identification stands in the place of a threatened or actual object loss (Freud, 1917, 1923a). Kate developed a marked proclivity to standing quietly about and taking in visually the activity of others, a characteristic of the mother but not heretofore noticeable in the child.

The major symptom at this time was a sleep disturbance, which during this period of development is a prototypic manifestation of the threat of object loss. The difficulty in falling asleep and the waking at night reflected the infant's struggle against the loosening of the tie to the object inherent in falling asleep, a struggle normal to this period, but exacerbated here by the actual experience of the loss of her father. Another cause of the sleep disturbance was the aggression that was mobilized by the threat of object loss. It was this intense aggression, we believe, that made it so difficult for the mother to comfort her child when she awoke from sleep in a panic.

An interesting sequel to the separation reaction and a final link to the subsequent castration reaction was the youngster's spontaneous and self-imposed bowel and bladder control. We are reasonably confident that beyond facilitating Kate's own spontaneous efforts, the mother did not in any important way influence the toilet training or impose it on her daughter. Kate was of course maturationally ready, but the impetus for the control of bowel and bladder arose out of the threat of object loss with which she was confronted at this time. With the self-imposed control of the toilet functions, she sought to hold onto and preserve the object. This evidence of the stool-object equation provides impressive testimony that the process of internalization and the establishment of the constancy of the object representation are clearly well advanced, and now the object as represented by the stool can be actively held onto or given up at will. A neat resolution, indeed, of the whole problem of threatened object loss. The achievement of object constancy, however, still has a way to go, since the relationship to the object is still highly ambivalent and the representation more concrete than abstract — that is, it is still related to the physical stool-object and is not yet entirely a mental process.

We are now in a position to understand the symptomatic triad of the castration reaction. The incontinence that developed would, in view of the foregoing considerations, indicate that the confrontation with the genital differences between the sexes was experienced not only as a threat to the body-self representation but as a threat of object loss. The sleep disturbance that followed reflects the same underlying content and must, in addition, be seen against the background of its earlier outbreak following the father's departure. Finally, the negativism bespeaks the intensely ambivalent relationship to the mother, ambivalence which is an amalgam of the enhanced dependence and the intense aggression mobilized by the threat of object loss.

And what about the shift in the youngster's responses to situations in which other children took something away from her or in some way interfered with her activity? Early in the course of the castration reaction, Kate seemed unable to tolerate such interference. At best, she obtained some solace in her mother's comforting, since there was little she could do to ease herself or in any way deal with the situation. The utter passivity she displayed was indeed striking. It is not difficult to see here a diffusion of the original noxious experience of her recognition of the anatomical genital difference. Kate's collapse reflects the severe narcissistic injury and undermining of the self representation consequent to the confrontation with the genital difference.

Kate's turning in furious attack when a child took anything away from her, some two months after the initial castration reaction, replacing her earlier passivity, was an aspect of a general change in her behavior: active reparative fantasies and behavior were much more in evidence than before. We saw indications of her belief that her mother and other grown women had a penis and that she might still grow one, as well as hints that the stool-phallus equation had been established and the underlying assumption that she had one. The hair-pulling suggests the presence of a well-developed syndrome of penis envy, with the aggressive impulse to seize the penis symbolized by the hair-pulling.

Of considerable interest was the voice of conscience that began to stir. This tiny conscience demonstrates the familiar self-observing function and speaks to the ego in a restraining fashion. Its incipient nature is reflected by its almost concrete tie to the object. The words are the mother's very own words, and its structure closely parallels the character of the underlying object representation in that its integrity is still very much subject to the vicissitudes of drive tension. That is to say, an independent and structured conscience does not yet exist, just as true object constancy has not yet been achieved.

In the foregoing description and discussion of a preoedipal castration reaction occurring in the latter half of the second year, we note the prominence of a sharp upsurge in object-loss anxiety, negativism, and an increased hostile dependence on the mother, behavioral currents very reminiscent of those Mahler describes as characteristic of the rapprochement crisis (Mahler et al., 1975). We believe that the apparently divergent explanations are complementary rather than contradictory. Mahler is of course fully aware of drive theory and cognitive development, but her focus is on object relations as a major organizer of early development. Our own explanatory system attempts to integrate object relations with drive (both sexual and aggressive) organization theory.

CHAPTER 2

THE EARLY GENITAL PHASE

Clinical data from the treatment of a pseudoautistic psychotic girl, Alice, led us to look for a place in our genetic constructions for the many observations of sexual arousal and activity that ran counter to earlier developmental concepts. Alice's behavior highlighted a number of features which ultimately suggested both the necessity and usefulness of proposing the existence of an early genital phase, for it increased our understanding of both aberrant patterns of development and important aspects of normal development.

ALICE

Alice was three and a half years old when she entered an intensive treatment program, as part of a research investigation of the separation-individuation phase in normal and psychotic children (see Mahler and Gosliner, 1955; Pine and Furer, 1963; Mahler and Furer, 1968; Mahler et al., 1975). She was well developed and physically attractive, except for a vacant, unfocused gaze and immobile features which gave her appearance a curiously unappealing quality.

Alice was a first-born child whose development, as we saw in retrospect, was already aberrant in the second half of the first year. Although her physical growth was entirely normal, her social responses were atypical. She was from very early on a sober-faced infant who very rarely smiled. When she awoke, either in the middle of the night or in the early morning, she never cried or called to her mother, but sat quietly in her crib until someone came to her. Even when she had an ear infection which on physical examination revealed an angry, red, bulging eardrum, she did not cry. By the end of the first year the pediatrician who had seen Alice since birth made the diagnosis of childhood autism. Although she did develop speech in the beginning of her second year, Alice did not appear to use it in a communicative fashion.

Her parents had separated when she was two years old. Thereupon her use of speech, such as it was, quickly diminished, so that when she appeared for treatment a year and a half later she was mute except for unintelligible vocalizations and shrieks. She was, at three and a half, incontinent and wore diapers both during the day and night. She never appeared to manifest any awareness of bowel and bladder functions, even when her mother made an effort to train her.

After the divorce, Alice's father, a boyish-looking, rather ineffectual young man in his late twenties who was probably a borderline character, maintained irregular contact with Alice in which he always seemed affectionate and gentle if somewhat vague. Alice's mother, a woman in her mid-twenties, was of considerable intellectual achievement. She remarried soon after her divorce and by the time Alice was five had two other children who seemed, as best as we could tell, to be bright, attractive, and normal youngsters. She managed these two infants and the difficult older psychotic child quite effectively, without much domestic help. In her handling of Alice, however, she frequently seemed to be somewhat detached and often asserted wryly that our efforts would come to naught since she believed Alice was organically damaged. Such remonstrances seemed less an evidence of her rejection of the child than a reflection of the profound narcissistic insult and sense of guilt which compelled her to insist that the child was organically damaged rather than compromised as a result of inadequate mothering.

While Alice was largely oblivious to her human environment unless it impinged too closely or vigorously upon her, she carried with her everywhere a burdensome collection of plastic baby bottles, a shredded blanket, and a toy duck, objects from which she could not bear to be parted. Her activity alternated between an aimless wandering and a concentrated and almost endlessly repetitive filling and emptying of her baby bottles with dried peas or dirt painstakingly collected from crevices in the concrete-floored playground.

After several months of work with her therapist, Alice began to show some cracks in her autistic shell. She began to use the therapist to fetch objects that were out of reach, to join in mutual rhythmic play, and occasionally burrowed in her therapist's embrace in a relaxed, dreamy, infantile attitude.

In this general climate of object involvement, Alice was one day observed frantically running about the playroom with a searching, darting gaze, as if she were looking for something. She suddenly stopped, her gaze focused; she momentarily strained at a bowel movement and then resumed running about as before. Previously, Alice had not manifested even the slightest awareness of bowel or bladder functions, nor had she shown any observable behavioral reflections of these functions. When it was pointed out to her that she was looking for something outside of herself, when, in fact, what she was responding to was the inner stimulus of bowel urgency, Alice flew into a panic tantrum of awesome dimensions. From that time on it was possible, in an emotionally meaningful climate, to delineate interpretively for Alice such primitive ego discriminations as inside-outside, self-nonself, animate-inanimate. In the process, the behavioral concomitants of and her attitudes toward the bowel urgency became sharply focused in a well-defined sequence of cause and effect such as had never before been observed in her autistically organized state. For a time the sequence of bowel urgency-interpretation-panic tantrum became much more frequent, so that the several hours Alice spent daily at the treatment center were entirely consumed in the most intense conflict over holding on and letting go of her stool. Gradually she seemed to resolve the conflict by withholding her bowel movement until nighttime, when she was asleep in her bed wearing diapers.

As the conflict over bowel urgency receded, behavior and conflict very similar in many details, at least at the outset, were manifested around urinary urgency. Much the same interpretive ground was covered as was the case with the bowel conflict. Naturally, the polarities of self-nonself and inside-outside were traversed in a much more telescoped fashion. During this phase of the treatment, her attention seemed almost constantly to be riveted to her bladder and she wet herself two, three, or four times in a morning. In this respect she seemed very much like a normal youngster in the midst of her bladder training in that the urgency seemed so marked and so frequent. It was only in the extreme intensity of the profound anxiety she experienced that one could see the difference. When Alice was anxiously beset with the sensations of a full bladder, she would drink water so that her cheeks literally bulged with the retained liquid. When she could no longer contain the urinary urgency and wet herself, she would swallow the mouthful of water, occasionally also dribbling some of it from her mouth, a happy enough compromise for this youngster who could not bear to incur the loss of part of her body content. While she ultimately could not control the discharge of the bladder to the outside, the other cavity, the mouth bulging with water, could be controlled and could be made to empty into the inside of the body.

With the gradual withholding and achievement of control of the urinary function, a new developmental feature arose which is central to the formulation of an early genital phase. As Alice became increasingly able to withhold the immediate discharge of bladder contents, she began for the first time to manifest unmistakable and unambiguous indications of genital arousal. For the first time she was observed to masturbate openly, and she began to examine the genital area of the playroom dolls with extraordinary curiosity and concentration. There were also signs of a developing penis-envy syndrome. She was seen to interrupt her masturbation and dart into the adjoining playroom of a young boy, where she would steal his model airplane, his car, or toy soldiers, and return to her room in an excited and euphoric mood.

In view of the foregoing, we draw the general inference that, with the delay in the immediate discharge of bowel and bladder tension in the early phase of establishing toilet control, a spread in excitation to and arousal of the genital organs regularly and normally occurs. This seems to be a neurophysiological maturational sequence. It would also appear that, after several months of more firmly established mastery of sphincter control, what follows is a loosening in the association of sphincter, rectal, and bladder tension, on the one hand, and genital arousal, on the other. The genitals have now sufficiently matured to serve as a channel for discharge and as a source for the sensation of pleasure. This series of developments supports the thesis that postulates the occurrence of castration reactions at this early age in that it establishes the conditions for the high narcissistic cathexis of the genitals indicated by such reactions.

As already noted, the genital arousal, which is a central aspect of this phase, is a developmental precipitate, so to speak, of the whole process of sphincter control. The clinical sketch of Alice's developmental progress in her therapy described how her relationship to her own stool paralleled and was directly bound up

with the level of her own object relations. The first behavioral reflection of a bowel movement was manifested only after the months of therapeutic work had
forged a relatively solidly established need-satisfying relationship with her therapist. While Alice could periodically retreat into her autistic shell, she was just as often
driven outward again by her object hunger. From this
time onward, the stool, the concrete symbol of her oral
attachment to the nourishing object, could no longer
pass through her body without psychic registration because her attachment to the object, her therapist, had
provided the necessary ingredient for advancement in
her ego capacities.

Confirmation that the stool-object equation had
been formed came from the mother's own report. Beginning at this period, whenever Alice's mother
momentarily had to leave Alice alone in the bath to tend
to some immediate household requirement, Alice had a
bowel movement in the bath. At first, she would complete ignore the stool on her mother's return. However,
when her relationship with her mother had become
warmer, she would pick up the stool with a beaming
smile and offer it to her mother in the friendliest
fashion.

The experience of passing the bowel movement
was for this child clearly equivalent to her mother's
leaving her and, we think, reflects the sense of depletion
of the self created by the separation. The early total ignoring of the stool on the mother's return bespeaks
Alice's obliterating anger at being left, in much the
same way as the hospitalized child's nonrecognition of
the returning mother reflects the rage at being aban-

doned. The later friendly proffering of the stool to the returning mother bespeaks the growing warmth of her object relations as well as a greater tolerance for separation.

Our experience with Alice offers interesting, although inexact parallels to the normal infant's developing relation to his bowel movement. Early in the first year, the infant tends to have his or her stool during feedings or shortly thereafter, and usually pays no attention to and manifests no behavioral reflection of the passage of the bowel movement. Toward the end of the first year and certainly early in the second, we commonly see a tendency to a certain general body rigidity, some straining, not infrequently a brief stilling of other body activity, and withdrawal of attention from the outside as the stool is passed. Furthermore, it is a commonplace with our normal 14- to 15-month-old toddlers to note their sudden fascination with the toilet and particularly the flush, and their highly excited and absorbed observation of the disappearance of the stool, toilet paper, or a toy as it is flushed down the toilet.

This shift in the infant's attitude to his own bowel movement seems to follow the normal and, at this age, typical emergence of a separation conflict, with all this implies about increasing stability of the self and object representations. Until eight or nine months, the infant's differentiation of itself appears to be extremely rudimentary and the relation to the object essentially a symbiotic one. With the onset of the differentiation subphase, there is a rapid quickening in the whole process of the establishing of the sense of self, particularly the body self, and the psychological sense of separation of the infant from his mother (Mahler, 1963; Mahler and

Furer, 1968). It is at this stage, with the new level of self and object differentiation, that the bowel movement is singularly situated and suited to express the developing double-faced inner concept of something that is part of the self and that at the same time can be felt outside. It has a movement and yet is not alive, has a climactic expulsive pattern of release, a texture, a smell, and a very intimate and important relationship to the nourishing object; yet when expelled, it is neither self nor object.

The stool's movement, texture, and consistency are subject to the vicissitudes of health and sickness. It is affected by loving and hating feelings toward the object in that rage at the object frequently results in diarrhea, while efforts to preserve the stool-object in the face of such anger frequently results in constipation. The ultimate control of the bowel function waits on some partial resolution of the separation conflicts, the independence conflicts, and the conflicts over self-dissolution and object loss. The infant's newly emergent attention to the bowel movement and his new relation to it follows from and is a reflection of the developing self and object relationships. In this sense, the infant's attitude toward his bowel function is quite independent of any demand from the parents, either explicit or implicit, for control of this function. In fact, the reasonably well-attuned parent will wait for the emergence of this naturally occurring shift in the infant's own relationship to his stool, taking the cue from the infant as to when to support and encourage this new and developing control, with all that this implies in relation to the developing sense of self and object.

The early evidence of bowel patterning in Alice has

already been described. As work with the bowel conflict proceeded, the patterning effects of the bowel movements on a variety of ego functions became richer and more comprehensive. She began, under the influence of bowel urgency, to gather into a pile toys from all over the playroom and later built towers of 10 blocks or more. The first time she successfully built a tower of blocks, she shrieked in exultation, "I can do it!" This was the first time she had ever uttered a complete sentence or had ever referred to herself as "I." The tower-building became for quite some time an absolute indication that she was experiencing bowel urgency. Her body posture at these times regularly showed a good deal of rigidity and her body movements were very stiff. Clearly, the block-building, the toy-gathering, the postural rigidity and stiffness of movement all reflected the inner muscular tension and perhaps even the column of stool.

For many months thereafter, the conflict of feelings concerning the stool-object raged; Alice could not ignore it and she could not resolve it. Painstaking interpretive work dealt with a variety of reincorporative and destructive fantasies. The panic centered essentially around the threat of object loss and the related threat to the integrity of the self. With the partial working through of these conflicts, Alice's increasing ego capacity, as manifested in her gradually improving sphincter control, was enhanced. Much of this was touchingly confirmed when Alice had her first bowel movement in the toilet. With this loss she developed for the first time a profound sadness, a sadness which could be empathically recognized as such and which lasted for several days.

It may be said that a relationship inferred from the highly chaotic and atypical development of a psychotic child cannot have relevance for normal development. We maintain, however, that the study of the severe neuroses and the psychoses may serve to focus for us many features of very early development, just as the study of the transference neurosis served to clarify the importance of the later oedipal constellation in normal development. Certainly, there have been precedents for such a view. Mahler's hypothesis of the normal separation-individuation phase developed from her studies of symbiotic psychosis (Mahler and Gosliner, 1955), Lewin's confirmation of his dream-screen thesis (1946) was drawn from the dream of a schizophrenic patient, and Freud's thinking on early normal narcissism arose in the context of investigating the psychoses (Freud, 1911).

The association of anal sensations with genital sensations is by no means a novel observation. Freud (1933) wrote, "there are a few isolated reports of early vaginal sensations as well, but it could not be easy to distinguish these from sensations in the anus or vestibulum" (p. 188). And Jones (1927) stated, "The anus is evidently identified with the vagina to begin with, and the differentiation of the two is an extremely obscure process, more so perhaps than any other in female development; I surmise, however, that it takes place in part at an earlier age than is generally supposed" (p. 443). Brunswick (1940) also called attention to vaginal sensitivity arising early and associated with anal stimulation.

Greenacre (1950) anticipated many of our findings without quite making the association of a regularly occurring early genital phase. She found evidence of very early vaginal awareness, hazy and unverified though it is. And she addressed the issue of preoedipal genital sexuality when she stated her belief that genital stimulation may occur much earlier than the phallic stage when the infant is under conditions of extreme stress (1970). In such cases, Greenacre noted, there may be a diffusing of tension into systems not quite mature, resulting in a premature functioning of the genital apparatus. From observations made in patients with pathological sexual development, she found that vaginal awareness was more prominent in patients who had been subjected in infancy to repeated stimulation of the rectum and anus. When this stimulation had occurred before the phallic phase, a strong oral-vaginal response developed in reaction to primal-scene observations.

A major developmental precipitate of the early genital phase is the integration of the genital representation into the concept of the body. Loewenstein (1950, pp. 47–48), in a charming observational vignette, which we have in several instances been able to confirm, described a 10-month-old boy's discovery of his penis and the whole process of his experimental confirmation that his penis belonged to his body. At this level, the integration of the genital into the body self, as he described it, is mediated through tactile, kinesthetic, and, most important, visual incorporation. The importance of the visual mode for this level of genital integration into the body image must, incidentally, play a small role at best for the little girl, inasmuch as she cannot readily see her own genitals. In any case, we think the contribution of this level of experience to the ultimate genital schematization — that is, to the psychic representation of the genitals — must be weak indeed. We therefore take exception to Loewenstein's assertion that the boy's castration anxiety in the phallic phase "takes as its model" the infantile uncertainty that the penis is an indissoluble part of his own body, that is, if Loewenstein meant that there is a dynamic relationship between the two, as he seemed to suggest.

We believe that the central importance of the early genital phase for the gradual establishment of genital schematization rests on the fact that a normal and regularly occurring genital arousal occurs during this phase, and this implies that the genitals have matured sufficiently to serve as a channel for tension discharge and pleasure possibility.

Freud (1905) originally conceptualized the sequence of the emergence of the erotogenic zones as a biologically predestined, regularly occurring process of maturation. Greenacre (1953a) offered a modification of this concept, suggesting that all three erotogenic zones may be active to some degree from birth onward; the peaks of ascendancy of each zone, however, would follow a maturational timetable. Furthermore, Greenacre suggested that any zone might be prematurely activated by the infant's life experience.

The major thrust of development up to this point has been the differentiation of the self from the object and the internalization and solidification of the object representation as signaled in the achievement of sphincter control. We are proposing that this achievement leads to the developmental precipitate of genital arousal, which heralds the onset of an early genital phase. At this juncture, the specific anxieties of the two contiguous phases, object loss and castration, are indissoluble. We believe that the later castration anxiety of the phallic phase is genetically linked to that of the early genital phase, and, by virtue of this, has a direct developmental connection to the anxiety of object loss. Freud (1926) discussed the relation between the anxieties of object loss and castration. While our investigations have shown that this relationship is an actual and developmentally prototypic one, the castration anxiety in the phallic phase no longer has the direct and immediate resonance of object loss that it had in the earlier genital phase. In the intervening period, the object representation has become further solidified and the constancy of the representation is to a larger extent insured.

As already stated, a thesis that explains early castration reactions requires that the conditions leading to the high narcissistic cathexis of the genitals implied in such reactions be established. This condition has been satisfied by postulating a normal and regularly occurring genital arousal at this early age, with the implied maturation of the genitals as a channel for the discharge of tension and the possibility of pleasure.

It is our belief that the concept of an early genital phase helps to account for the phenomena of the narcissistic injury and the undermining of the self representation that result from the perception of the anatomical difference between the sexes. In this sense, the situation is similar to that of the phallic-phase child who is traumatized by his observation of the sexual difference precisely because there is such a high narcissistic evaluation of the genitals during the phallic phase as well. In the cases from the Hampstead Nursery, described in Chapter 1, in which violent penis-envy reactions in little girls were observed in the second half of the second year, Anna Freud similarly felt that the responsible factor may have been the observation of the genitals of children of the opposite sex. In Sach's cases of severe castration anxiety, the provocative experiences were not delineated, but it seems safe to infer that the mother had been observed urinating and been seen not to possess a penis.

Another feature to be noted in these cases was the clustering of the reported castration reactions between the ages of 18 and 24 months. This is, of course, the age range in which at least preliminary sphincter control is ordinarily established, and with it the consequent genital arousal.

The observations we have described in this and the preceding chapter led us to propose certain emendations to the theory of early drive development. We decided that our ideas could best be tested by directly observing normal children during their second year of life. To this end, in 1967, a research program was established under the auspices of the Department of Child Psychiatry of the Albert Einstein College of Medicine. As a result of this research, we found it necessary to revise some of our original ideas. In the chapters that follow, we describe the research program and detail the findings that required modifications in our original hypothesis.

We are now proposing the existence of a normal and regularly occurring early genital phase starting sometime between the 15th and 24th month. This phase runs concomitantly with the infant's increasing ability to differentiate self from object; it occurs in both boys and girls and appears to be without any oedipal resonance. The underlying dynamic content of the early genital phase is normally concerned with establishing self and object representations, which now include the genital zone. From the onset of the early genital phase, all of the infant's major experiences will have a genital reflection.

We are further proposing that, with early genital arousal and the infant's perception of the anatomical difference between the sexes, castration reactions will develop, especially if the infant has earlier in life been subjected to experiences that interfered with the developing sense of body intactness or with the mother-child relationship and thus produced an instability of self and object representations. These castration reactions will vary in intensity and form, depending on the infant's previous experiences in the specific areas just mentioned.

Finally, we are proposing that the particular manner in which the infant negotiates this early genital phase will exert a decisive influence upon the nature of the child's sense of sexual identity.

The development of sexual interest and activities which we have outlined constitutes an early genital phase rather than a less organized aspect of increasing genital awareness for the following reasons. First, it occurs in a regular developmental sequence, except when early strain has been of such proportions as to interfere with the normal differentiation process. Second, not

only is endogenous genital sensitivity remarkably increased, but psychological awareness of the genitals has
now been attained and the infant shows a regular and
persistent curiosity, visual and tactile, about his or her
own genitals as well as those of other children and
adults. Third, this new type of sexual interest and activity affects all areas of functioning.

The task of documenting the sequence of psychosexual development through direct observation of infants has emerged as an important basic problem con-
fronting psychoanalytically oriented researchers during
the past decade or more. The first systematic psychoanalytic studies of early genital activity, carried out by
Spitz and Wolf (1949), concerned mothers and infants
living in a penal institution. Anna Freud's and Dorothy
Burlingham's observations, referred to earlier, were also
confined to infants in institutions. In contrast to these,
Kleeman (1965, 1966) reported on a mother's direct observation of her infant son's developing genital self-
stimulation.

Our research was aimed at first-hand observations
of normal children living at home with their parents.
Our intention was to investigate the existence of an early phase of sexual interest and activity as well as deviations and distortions in this phase. We therefore included among our normal subjects infants whom we knew
had had some previous experience that might have
interfered to some degree with developing self and object representations.

CHAPTER 3

THE RESEARCH NURSERY
AND THE PROGRAM

When we set up our research nursery we were most fortunate in having been familiar with the Masters Children's Center developed by Margaret S. Mahler (1963: see also Pine and Furer, 1963; Mahler et al., 1975), which we used as our model. Modifications were necessary because of the difference in the aims of the two projects. Whereas Mahler and her co-workers studied the separation-individuation process with regard to developing object relations, our research focused on psychosexual development and aggression as they were intertwined with other aspects of development, especially object relations and cognition.

The nursery was located in a small four-story building away from the hospital itself. The nursery room (see Figure 1) measured roughly 24 by 30 feet and comfortably accommodated the eight or nine mothers

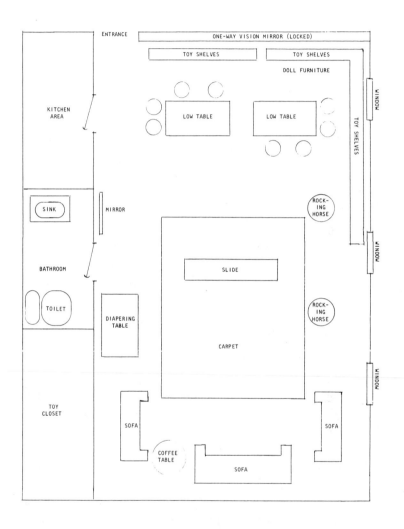

FIGURE 1

and infants, which was the usual complement to appear on any given morning, along with two teachers and the staff of participant-observers.

(The senior and junior staff members assigned to each mother-infant pair each attended a different session during the week, as will be described below, thus providing a larger observational data base.) Mild intercurrent illnesses or family matters usually kept at least one or two infants from the nursery each session.

Leading directly from the room was the entrance to a small kitchen where snacks were prepared and bottles and clothing stored, and along that same wall was the entrance to a full-size home-style bathroom. On the opposite side, windows looked out onto a quiet, middle-class residential street. In addition to a slide, two rocking horses, a large-sized doll's bed, and several doll carriages, the room contained open shelves filled with toys. There were also low tables and chairs for the infants where they could play or have their snacks. At the opposite end was an informal grouping of sofas and a table for the mothers.

We tried to make the setting as natural as possible. Although a one-way mirror extended along one of the end walls of the nursery room, with an observational booth behind it, the entrance to this booth was locked during the nursery sessions, and the mothers were so informed. No movies or videotapes were taken during nursery sessions, except on a few special occasions such as birthday parties when filming was done very much in the manner one would photograph a family gathering. (These films were shown to the parents at the party held for them at the close of each nursery year.) It was our impression that our strict adherence to the restrictions against the possibility of being observed without their knowledge allowed for a far greater naturalness in the behavior of mothers, infants, and staff members.

During the sessions, the mothers usually sat at their end of the room watching the children, coming to their aid at times in an entirely free and natural way, talking to each other or to a member of the staff, or sipping coffee, as if they were in an indoor playground.

Toys included some dolls, two of which were made with genitally accurate bodies; a dollhouse with furniture and utensils; crayons and paper; and a wide variety of toys chosen because of their resemblance to the various body orifices. A particular favorite was the shape box, a wooden box with a hinged lid containing openings through which a circular, triangular, or square piece of wood could be fitted, dropped, and then retrieved from within the box. (Although our nursery school teachers knew that infants of this age loved to play with the shape box, they didn't recognize its structural similarity to anal functioning until this was pointed out to them.) Another favorite — also connected with anal interests — was the play-dough machine, a plastic toy with an opening through which the infant could insert play-dough. Pressing a lever against the play-dough forces the extrusion of an elongated segment of dough. The toddlers' use of the slide provided us with clues about emerging fear of heights, as well as fears concerning loss of both anal and urinary control.

The view from the windows added to the naturalism we were aiming for: the street was very much like the streets the infants were already familiar with. Window sills were a place for retreat, for fantasy, for evocations of daddy when a car passed by.

The bathroom was another favorite place. The infants had free access to its sink, flush toilet, and two child commodes, although a teacher always accompanied any youngster who ventured there, for the room was cut off from general view both by its position and by a regular door which could be closed. Everything— dolls, toys, bottles—was thrown into the toilet during the course of the year; indeed, our plumbing bills were astronomical.

The diapering table was deliberately placed just outside the door to the bathroom, in full view of the people in the nursery. If the observation of the diapering which took place at frequent intervals was stimulating, it was equally stimulating to all the infants. By the same token, whatever limitations might have been imposed by being observed were the same for all.

The Staff

Although our head teacher and her assistant, both trained nursery school teachers, were always there to supervise, the mothers were expected to take care of their own babies. The presence of the teachers left the observers free to observe the infants or to interact with them and their mothers. The senior observers (ourselves and other members of the faculty) attended at least one session a week, though not on the same day. We did not find the absence of consensual observation to be a disadvantage; on the contrary, when we compared notes we found that we had often observed the same phenomena, since they tended to continue over a period of days or even weeks. Continuity of observation was assured by the presence of junior observers — residents or fellows in child psychiatry, pediatrics, or psychology — on the days a senior observer was not in attendance. As already mentioned, each mother-infant pair was observed at least twice weekly. These observations were further augmented by observations and reports from the teachers. The teachers were oriented in advance regarding the aim of the study and were encouraged to describe incidents that occurred when the observers were not at hand.

THE SUBJECTS

Seventy infants and their families participated in our study between September, 1968 and July, 1975. Four cases studied in the first year had to be deleted because of incomplete data, leaving a sample of 66 cases, which constituted our data base. The sample was exactly divided between the sexes.

Fifty-four of our infants were first-borns, of whom 24 acquired younger siblings subsequently. Only one toddler had both an older and younger sibling at the time of our initial informal follow-up, which took place soon after the project closed. Of the 24 infants who acquired a sibling, 14 acquired one of the same sex. Fifteen of these younger siblings were born before our subjects had attained their second birthday. This proved to be significant in that the maternal relationship became attenuated to varying degrees and appeared to affect both the progress of separation-individuation and the subject's reaction to the onset of the early genital phase.

We, nevertheless, do not believe that this sample is large enough to provide a reliable basis for conclusions regarding the effect of sibling position on the developmental issues mentioned.

Roughly two-thirds of the infants were from upper-middle-class families, the rest from lower-middle-class families, and all but two of the families were white. That our research population was fairly homogeneous resulted from the nature of our initial recruiting, which had been conducted at the local hospital playground, through talking to new members of the hospital staff, and by the hospital "grapevine." The mothers who volunteered the first year were largely of the upper-middle class, and insofar as one group recommended the next group over each succeeding year, the socioeconomic level of the group tended to remain the same throughout the years, although several families came from a nearby low- to middle-income housing development.

The majority of the fathers were engaged in medical or related hospital programs, while the mothers' educational levels ranged from that of high school graduate to postgraduate degrees of various kinds. While some of the mothers worked part time, all of them were the primary caretakers of their children during their first two years. The homogeneity of the sample served to highlight individual differences in personality and child-rearing attitudes, and differences in the "style" of both parents and infants in handling the typical events of the second year of life; it also resulted in reducing the variables of this sample.

The parents were told in advance by one of the directors or the head nursery teacher that we were engaged in research having to do with normal development during the second year of life, that we were interested in learning the particulars about how boys and girls begin to differ and how babies begin to play. We explained that we would expect each mother and her infant to attend a two-hour session four mornings a week from September through June.

The babies were between 10 and 13 months old when they actually entered the nursery. From the pool of self-selected families who were interested in attending the nursery, two babies, a boy and a girl, were deliberately chosen each year on the basis of their having had, during the first year of life, some experience that would be expected to predispose them to the occurrence of a preoedipal castration reaction.

Eight of our total sample of 33 girls were preselected because they suffered from at least one of the following conditions: congenital hip dislocation (one subject), a serious postpartum maternal depression (two subjects), serious but not life-threatening parental physical illness (two subjects), "failure to thrive" syndrome (one subject), severe and prolonged sleep disturbance and constipation (one subject), and one subject born five weeks prematurely who had severe early colic and diarrhea.

Ten infant boys were preselected out of the total sample of 33 boys because they had experienced one of the following situations: four of the boys were nonidentical twins, one boy had been adopted, one had bilateral clubbed feet and a disturbed relationship with his mother, one boy's father was away from home during most of the infant's first and second years, two had mothers who had suffered serious postpartum depressions, and one infant had serious difficulties in regard to the mother-child relationship.

The other babies were, as far as could be determined from their initial history, free from any such experience. We found, however, that many of the infants in our randomly selected sample had also had unusual first-year experiences, although we learned about these only after the infants were participating in our study. This information had been deliberately withheld in some instances, while other parents had simply not thought of relating these experiences, so much were they part of the very fiber of the parents' lives. Still others had repressed the memory of the experiences, only to have them re-emerge as their relationships with our observers deepened or as subsequent events stirred up these forgotten memories. This is an aspect of all research material gathered retrospectively. As we became aware of this factor, we altered our research design: we began to interview babies and their parents when the babies were five or six months old.

However, even this earlier access to developmental and family material was not a wholly satisfactory solution. The parents simply were not aware of many aspects of their own behavior and feelings and significant family events, and therefore could not be expected to describe them. Not until they entered the nursery program did we gain access to much of the infants' and parents' past experiences as they were then recalled by the parents as part of each day's history-taking.

Finally, it should be mentioned that many life

events, both ordinary and extraordinary, influenced the development of our subjects in the course of our studying them. Illness, the death of a grandparent or other significant family members, as well as many other occurrences, constituted yet another variable which had somehow to be taken into account as we analyzed the data.

THE PROCEDURE

In late spring and summer of each year, recruiting began for the following autumn. The infants were then between seven and 10 to 11 months of age. In the third year of the program's operation, when we had refined our procedures sufficiently, the head teacher or a senior observer visited the infant's home for the initial interview, thus providing an informal setting where information could be elicited under more casual circumstances and first-hand observations of the home settings could be made. Table 1 (see pp. 52–58) shows the categories used for guiding these initial interviews, although the interviews were never carried out in a formal manner. We also took the histories of the parents in as casual a way as possible, enlisting the help of the infant's grandparents during chats when they visited their grandchildren in the nursery. Such informal history-gathering yielded valuable information about the parents' childhood and development.

To organize the collection of the ongoing data, category sheets were used as a guide, and these sheets then constituted the basis for our flow charts (see Table 2, p. 59). The flow charts provided two valuable profiles; when read vertically, the child's development in several sectors could be correlated at that given moment; when read horizontally, the ongoing developmental process in any area could be traced. In addition to these general categories, observers and teachers were provided with detailed guidelines (see Tables 3–6, pp. 60–68) for recording information regarding anal, urinary, and genital behavior, and the use of transitional objects; these guidelines also accounted for play behavior.

While the nursery program was in session, the observer questioned the mother informally about the infant's behavior at home during the interval since the previous interview, making sure that certain preselected behavioral categories were covered during that interview. The observer spent the remainder of the nursery session directly observing the infant, recording a narrative account of the infant's behavior over a period of 10 minutes, and also interacting with the infant. At the end of the session, the observer dictated an impressionistic account of the entire session. We were particularly careful about indicating the source of the data (whether direct or from a mother), any discrepancies between mother's reports and nursery observations, and noting expected behavior that failed to take place.

Research evidence in our study consisted of patterns of behavior that recurred repetitively, and clusters of behavior from which we inferred a relationship to common underlying mental content. Behavior here includes play behavior. Verbal accompaniment or verification is usually not available until well into the latter part of the second year, except in precocious children. These clusters and patterns of behavior derived from direct observation were collected for all the children, and we correlated this direct observational data with the material relevant to ego and drive development obtained from the mother. For example, it was possible to trace behavior originally carried out on the infant's body or on the mother's body as it became externalized to the inanimate world. Touching or probing of the anus, interest in the soiled diaper, and toilet flushing gave way to interest in garbage cans, garbage trucks, and openings in walls and fences.

Play behavior was an important indicator of development of the body image and object relations, and was studied for its structural nature as well as for its content. By this we mean that similarities in patterning or organizational characteristics were noted, although the actual play content might have differed. For example, a child in the throes of anal-zone preoccupation demonstrated the anal qualities of pushing and filling and emptying with a variety of diverse objects. Often the choice of the object was guided more by its structural properties than by any of its other attributes.

Our frequent contact with the parents facilitated the establishment of a rather close relationship with them. We could evaluate with a fair degree of conviction the accuracy of their reports of their infant's and their own behavior and attitudes, and were also able to gauge the affective atmosphere in which these infants were being reared. Although our findings were based on data gathered largely from observing the children in a nonhome setting, watching the baby jointly with the mother as we sat chatting with her often elicited spontaneous descriptions of behavior at home or elsewhere.

And even within the nursery setting, many one-to-one intimate interchanges between mother and baby frequently occurred and could be observed and recorded.

Nevertheless, because we recognized that the infant's behavior is different in the presence of a group of people and away from home, in our fourth year of operation we instituted home-visit observation as a complement to observations made in the nursery itself.

Every two to three months the two observers assigned to each mother-infant pair prepared summaries of their case, again according to the preselected categories. Our flow charts (see Table 2) provided the material for these summaries, which were precirculated among the entire staff in order to facilitate discussion of them at our weekly staff conferences. Our theoretical and clinical formulations grew out of the discussions at these weekly staff conferences.

Both the mothers and the children became very much attached to the members of the staff, particularly to their own observers. The staff in turn exercised considerable tact and self-control in order to maintain a comfortable ambience. The interviews carried out in the homes — supplements to the nursery observations — were structured so as to take on the air of a casual discussion: "How is she today? What's new?" or, "You went out; how did she take to the new baby-sitter? How was she when you came home?"

We found that the mothers' attachment to the senior observers contained unmistakable transference elements. As parental figures, we were frequently asked the questions most young parents ask about their children. The more casual of these questions were answered, but for anything that was felt to be more serious we recommended that the parents speak to their own pediatrician.

It might have been simply a function of the varying ages of our staff members, but we found that the senior staff represented parental figures, and the teacher was often viewed as an aunt. The junior observers and assistant teachers, however, seemed to be regarded as peers, and were invited to dinner and to outings with the family, unlike the other staff members.

TABLE 1

CATEGORIES FOR RECORDING INITIAL DATA

1. **Pregnancy**
    Nature
    Difficulties
    Planned or not
    Sexual preference
    How or when name chosen
    Whether contraceptives were used, and if so, for
        how long

2. **Birth**
    Premature or late
    Delivery
    Length
    Nature
    Hospital
    Birthweight
    Mother's physical condition postpartum
    Mother's emotional condition postpartum
    Apgar score
    Brazelton testing

3. **Neonatal Period**
    Difficulties in breathing
    Nature of feeding
    Excessive crying
    Length of hospital stay
    Quality of early days at home
    Mother's emotional and physical condition

4. **Feeding History**
    Bottle or breast

Nature of schedule
Description of feedings
Use of pacifier
Solids
Self-feeding, when initiated
Thumb-sucking
Difficulties
    Vomiting
    Regurgitation
    Colic
    Diarrhea
    Constipation
    Medication or procedures used

5. Sleeping History
    Location
    Nature
    Rituals
    Special soothing methods (see Transitional Object
        category below)
    Regularity
    Disturbances

6. Motor Development: ages at which the following
occurred
    Head held up
    Sitting up with and without support
    Standing
    Crawling
    Walking with and without support
    Small muscle coordination — pincer grasp, general
        nature

7. Social Developmental Events
Smile
>First appearance
>Special for mother

Recognition of mother as a special person, or father as a special person

Stranger anxiety (when, intensity, circumstances)

Other fears
>Loud noises
>Men's faces and voices
>Vacuum cleaners

Separation anxiety
>When
>Intensity
>Circumstances
>Preparation by mother or other

8. Communication
Gestural
>Yes/no head-shaking
>Waving bye-bye

Verbal
>Cooing, babbling, vocalization
>First words
>Mama
>Papa
>Naming of other objects

9. Aggressive Behavior
Unfocused (irritability and restlessness)

Focused
>Hitting
>Biting

Scratching
Spitting
Throwing
Smearing
Kicking, etc.

10. Separation Experiences
Circumstances
Maternal substitutes
Reaction of child
Duration
Illness occurring in reaction to

11. Imitative Behavior
Direct or deferred
Of whom
Type

12. Reaction to:
Hair cuts
Nail cutting
Visits to pediatricians
Inoculations
Physical trauma

13. Medical History
Type of illnesses and operations, including convulsions, trauma, asthma, allergic reactions, eczema, orthopedic device, etc.

Chronology of illnesses and hospitalizations and reactions to them

Attitude toward injury on part of infant and mother/father

14. **Play Behavior**
> Favorite toys
> Favorite reciprocal games with mother/father
> Earliest peek-a-boo and variety of peek-a-boo games
> Imitative use of parents' clothing
> Semisymbolic doll play
> (See also special types of play derivative of anal, urinary, and genital zones)

15. **Transitional Objects**
> Age initiated
> Nature of
> Obligatoriness
> Quality
> Parents' reaction

16. **Autogenous Behavior**
> Thumb-sucking
> Hair-pulling
> Self-stroking
> Self-rocking
> Self-biting
> Head-banging
> Tongue-pulling
> Eyelash-pulling, etc.

17. **Bathing and Diapering**
> Location
> Person who does them
> Reaction to
> Toys used as diversion
> Fears, excitement, and pleasure during
> Alone or with parents
> Reaction to hair-washing

18. **Toileting**
Parents'
Child's exposure to
Child's reaction to and comment on
Child's
When initiated
By whom
Location and device used (potty or commode, toilet)
Reaction to
Fears connected with
Specific words for functions and anatomical parts used by parents

19. **Genital Behavior**
Initial discovery of genitals
Chronology
Circumstances
Exploratory method used
Self-stimulation
Parents' reaction
Affective reaction of child
Masturbation
Autonomic reactions (rapid respiration, flushing, perspiration)

20. **Body Exploration** (other than genital, anal, and urinary)
Play with body parts of self or others (extremities, nose, eyes, ears, umbilicus)
Words used by parents, child to designate parts and functions
Mirror interest in self and others
Curiosity regarding parents' bodies (tactile, visual, verbal)

21. Home Visit

        Description of home (general furnishings, number
            of rooms, location of apartment or house)

        Does child have own room, bed, crib? If shared,
            with whom? Amount of confinement to crib?
            Playpen?

        Number of people living in home

        Grandparents

            Location of

            Relation to

        Other significant adults

TABLE 2
FLOW CHART

OBSERVERS:

NAME:
SEX:
DATE OF BIRTH:

	Week of: Age:	Week of: Age:	Week of: Age:	Week of: Age:
ORAL (including feeding)				
SLEEP				
ILLNESS				
MOTOR DEVELOPMENT				
PLAY				
TRANSITIONAL PHENOMENA				
LANGUAGE				
MISCELLANY (including life events)				
BODY EXPLORATION				
BODY SCHEMATIZATION				
ANAL-URINARY-GENITAL				
AFFECTS: LIBIDINAL				
AGGRESSIVE				
MOODS				
FEARS & ANXIETIES				
INTERACTION WITH OTHERS				
MOTHER				
FATHER				
OTHERS				

TABLE 3
ANAL-AWARENESS GUIDELINES

Note absence as well as presence of the following:

1. **Changes in Bowel Patterning**
   Diurnal variation
   Diarrhea
   Constipation
   Stool retention

2. **Behavior Preceding or Accompanying Defecation**
   Pulling at diaper
   Squatting
   Facial flushing
   Straining
   Grunting
   "Inward gaze"
   Cessation of other activities
   Hiding
   Sitting on toidy seat or toilet

3. **Behavior Following Defecation**
   Signaling for diaper change
   Smearing stool
   Eating stool
   Resisting diapering
   Hiding

4. **Affective Concomitants** (excitement, pleasure, shame, anxiety)

5. **Anal-Zone Exploration**
   Manual
   Using inanimate objects

6. **Parental Reaction**
   to above

7. **Toilet Training Efforts**
   Age
   Device used
   Location

8. **Anal Curiosity Regarding Parents, Other Adults, Siblings, Peers, Pets**
   Form and frequency
   Situation, including exposure to parents' and others' defecation
   Interest in toilet (flush, water, paper, soap, other)

9. **Derivative Anal Play**
   Interest in garbage cans, incinerator, garbage trucks
   Container interest and play (emptying and filling)
   "Collecting" behavior (dirt, toys, other)
   Doll play (simulating "toileting" of dolls, diapering)

10. **Affective Anal Derivatives**
    Aggression
       Diffuse (tantrums)
       Focused
          Smearing and messiness
          Scattering and banging, etc.
    "Negative" behavior, including "no"
    Shame related to defecation
    Anxiety related to defecation

11. **Verbalization Related to Defecation**
    Names supplied by parents
    Labeling and gesturing by infant
    Distortions in labeling by infant

TABLE 4
URINARY-AWARENESS GUIDELINES

Note absence as well as presence of the following:

1. **Changes in Urinary Patterning**
   Diurnal variation
   Urinary retention

2. **Behavior Preceding or Accompanying Urination**
   Pulling at diaper, other signaling
   Squatting
   "Inward gaze"
   Cessation of other activities
   Visual attention to area
   Control of stream (stopping and starting)
   Sitting on toidy or toilet

3. **Behavior Following Urination**
   Signaling for diaper change
   Hiding
   Resisting diapering

4. **Affective Concomitants** (excitement, pleasure, shame, anxiety)

5. **Urinary-Zone Exploration**

6. **Parental Reaction** to above

7. **Toilet Training**
   Timing
   Device used
   Location

Standing or sitting posture for boys encouraged

8. **Urinary Curiosity Regarding Parents, Other Adults, Siblings, Peers, Pets**
   Form and frequency
   Situation, including exposure to parents' and others' urination
   Parental reaction, including permission to touch
   Interest in toilet (flush, water, paper, soap, other)

9. **Derivative Urinary Play**
   Water play with faucets, hoses, watering cans, nipples, squirting
   Mouth water play (holding, squirting, spitting)
   Doll play (toileting, diapering)
   Interest in other urinary symbols (umbrella, fire hydrants, water "sounds")

10. **Verbalization Related to Urination**
    Names supplied by parent
    Gesturing and labeling by infants
    Distortion in labeling by infants

TABLE 5
GENITAL-AWARENESS GUIDELINES

1. **Specific Area of Genital Manipulation**
   Girls: mons, labia, clitoris, vagina
   Boys: penis, scrotum

2. **Nature of Genital Manipulation**
   Repetitive or not
   Rhythmic or not
   Quality (intensity, degree of vigor)
   Motion used (squeezing, pulling, rubbing)
   Body part used (hands, thighs), rocking, or strad-
      dling

3. **Context in which Manipulation Occurs**
   Physical
      Bathing
      Diapering
      Naked or clothed
      Crib, other
   Emotional (following frustration, anger, anxiety,
      other)

4. **Other Perceptual Modalities Simultaneously Involved**
   Visual (looking at genitals)
   Kinesthetic (rocking)

5. **Affective and Erotic Concomitants**
   Facial expression (pleasure, anxiety, guilt, anger)
   Autonomic nervous system signs (sweating, flush-
      ing, rapid respiration)

6. **Erections** — in boys

Presence or absence
Degree
Attention to

7. Simultaneous Involvement with Other Objects

Humans (parents, others)
   Visual (looks at, smiles at, other)
   Tactile (strokes, other)
Inanimate (use of bottle, toys, rocking horse, diaper, other) for masturbation
Animals (pets)

8. Mother's Reaction to Infant's Genital Manipulation

9. Sexual Reactions and Curiosity Regarding Parents, Other Adults, Siblings, Peers, Pets

Form (visual, tactile)
Frequency and intensity
Situation of exposure (primal scene, toilet, other)
Parental response, including permission to touch
Exposure to maternal menses
Inhibition of curiosity

10. Derivative Genital Behavior

Umbilicus
   Form
   Frequency
   Intensity
   Person involved
Play
   Dolls (inspection, exploration)
   Toy animals (inspection, exploration)
   Use of phallic-shaped objects for thrusting into holes, etc.

Verbalization
    Names used by parents for genitals
    Gesturing to genital area
    Labeling of genital area
    Distortions in labeling

TABLE 6

TRANSITIONAL-OBJECT GUIDELINES

1. **Nursing History**
   Breast
   Bottle, especially in bed at night, at naps, and use
   during day

2. **Pacifier History**

3. **Thumb- or Finger-Sucking History and Other Autogenous Behavior**

4. **Manipulation of Objects** (when sleepy or in bed)
   Sheets
   Blankets
   Self

5. **Auditory Rituals**
   Music box
   Other auditory repetitive stimuli

6. **Bedtime Routine**
   Held by mother until asleep
   Given bottle in crib
   Animals, toys, blankets in crib (use of, attention
   to)
   Obligatory quality of
   Sleep disturbance reactive to disturbance in
   Other behavior characteristic of bedtime or sep-
   aration

7. **Morning Routine**

8. Daily Behavior
     Carrying around house
     Use for comforting

9. Parents' Attitude Toward

CHAPTER 4

EARLY SEXUAL DEVELOPMENT AND OBJECT LOSS

Our experience leads us to believe that an endogenously rooted genital sexual current normally emerges early in the second year of life and, in interaction with object relations, becomes increasingly influential in organizing the infant's development, especially in forming the basic core of sexual identity. Early experiences that tend to challenge the infant unduly with the threat of object loss and body dissolution result in a faulty and fluctuating genital body image at a time when the infant is acquiring a concept of his own body.

Billy, whose longitudinal development we describe in this chapter, was one of the infants preselected because he had been subjected to experiences in his first year that would predispose him to manifesting a severe preoedipal castration reaction. In addition to experiencing two actual object losses, Billy had a mother excep-

69

tionally disposed to anxiety. The interference with the development of stable self and object representations led to a severe preoedipal castration reaction with the important sequelae of erotization of aggression and distortions in ego development.

BILLY

Billy was a sturdy, smiling little boy of 11 months, in the midst of his practicing subphase (Mahler et al., 1975) when he came to the nursery. He crawled everywhere, babbling as he went, investigating his surroundings and toys, showing relatively little anxiety over the strange setting and the many strange children and adults.

Billy's parents were a conscientious young couple in their late twenties. His father's work as a junior executive with a major oil company required that he be regularly and frequently absent throughout Billy's infancy; in addition, the father expected to be inducted into the army for overseas service sometime during Billy's first year. The threat of induction hung over the mother during her pregnancy, which was otherwise uneventful. Birth was normal. But the dread and foreboding of the impending induction notice continued until Billy was nine months old, when his father entered the army. The father remained away from the family until shortly before Billy's second birthday. Billy's development during his first year was reported to have been excellent, except for a sleep disturbance. He woke at least once and, not infrequently, three or four times during most nights. His mother was disturbed and anxious about this, even when he was only four weeks old and could hardly have been expected to sleep through the night. We suspect a connection existed between the sleep disturbance and the mother's anxiety.

When Billy first attended the nursery, he had been without his father for two months and had not, to the best of our knowledge, shown any direct reaction to his father's absence. Shortly after his first birthday he began to walk, and at 13 months he began to evidence mild but quite definite signs of separation anxiety, which became increasingly prominent in the next few months. Although he had formerly been left briefly from time to time with a relative or neighbor without becoming anxious, he now began to show decided uneasiness and apprehension at such times.

At this point Billy's mother reported that she had decided to leave the bathroom door open whenever she used the toilet in order to familiarize him with its use. Before this, she had regularly closed the door when she used the bathroom. Upon closer questioning it was apparent that Billy became anxious and could not tolerate this separation from his mother. (We have been surprised to learn how commonly parents of young children who have no regular domestic help leave the door open when they use the toilet.)

A particularly instructive description of Billy's reactions to separation when he was around 14 months old was afforded us when one of the neighbors, a young woman with whom he was quite familiar, was asked by his mother to sit with him in their own apartment while she ran some errands. Immediately after the mother left, Billy made for a plant in a corner of the living room and had to be restrained. He then wandered into his mother's bedroom, dreamily looked out the window, and called for his mother, clearly missing her. After being comforted by the sitter, he darted for an open bookshelf and began to tear one of his father's books. He was with some difficulty restrained from doing this. (Both activities were consistently forbidden Billy by his mother; usually a verbal restraint sufficed, but occasionally she slapped his hand when he was particularly insistent, as he was on this occasion.) After a short while he walked to his mother's night table, looking back at the sitter, who did not stop him. He put his hand toward the drawer and then pulled it out a little, again looking at her. Inferring that this must be a forbidden activity, she stopped him.

What did this behavior mean? Parents frequently must resort to sharp verbal prohibitions early in the child's second year, either to protect him or because they require an orderly house. Such admonitions, which serve as precursors in building up a superego, can produce remarkably persistent inhibitory effects.

More playful examples of defiance of the mother's prohibitions in her presence were displayed by Billy, and most of the other children in our nursery, on a number of occasions. For instance, Billy once reached for an electric wire and then coyly and expectantly looked at his mother. When the expected "no" was spoken, he chuckled and then, in high spirits, approached a forbidden bookcase, again looking archly back at his mother.

On the occasion of the incident with the night-table drawer, Billy became very cranky. The sitter picked him up, but this did not really comfort him. At his insistence, he was placed in his crib where he quickly found a pacifier he obviously knew was hidden there and put it into his mouth. He was then taken out of the crib, but after a few moments the sitter remembered that his mother did not like him to have the pacifier outside the crib and took it away from him. He became enraged and inconsolable until it was returned to him; then his mood changed, and he lay down on the couch next to the sitter. He began to play with the pacifier, taking it out of his mouth, chuckling, and putting it back in again, chewing on it and then spitting it out with his tongue; he continued thus for about five minutes until his mother returned.

Billy's playful defiance is ubiquitous in toddlers during their second year. It reflects the infant's maturing strivings for independence, modified by a still intense dependence on the mother. Such behavior seems to imply that the youngster has a will of his own. He is maturing because he is behaving in a way that looks forward to his becoming relatively autonomous. But he still expects and even invites his mother's disapproving response, thus showing his need for closeness and mutuality with her.

Billy's defiance when he was left with his sitter was more complex, however, in that he had to deal with an upsurge in anger at his mother for leaving him. We believe Billy, in his defiant behavior which both anticipated and required her response, was trying to evoke his mother's presence by magical-omnipotent means. He might have sought to evoke her presence in a number of other ways, but, angry with her for leaving him, he be-

haved in a way that defied her prohibitions and charac-
teristically elicited her disapproval. He was thereby
denying his longing through the implicit assertion that
he was independent and did not need her.

Billy had first attempted to deal with the separation by calling forth his most advanced, independent,
repertory of behavior. When this effort failed, there was
a sharp regression as evidenced by his resort to the
pacifier. Unable to call up the image of his mother in a
magical-omnipotent fashion by behavior that implied
reciprocal interaction with her, he turned to the pacifier
to evoke a fantasy of his mother's presence in a more
primitive and concrete way. In removing the pacifier
and chuckling, it was he who abandoned the object
rather than being abandoned; in his chewing and spitting out of the pacifier, he clearly demonstrated his
angry rejection of the object.

During the next two months numerous incidents
reflected Billy's conflict over separation. On several
occasions at the end of a nursery session, he looked apprehensive as he saw another mother and child leave the
nursery, and ran crying to the open door. Under ordinary circumstances Billy could of course discriminate
between his mother and the other adults in the nursery.
However, as he became anxious over separation he
reacted to some other woman's departure as if she were
his own mother.

When Billy was a little older than 14 months he developed, in the nursery and at home, a series of games
which involved his ears, eyes, and mouth. At first he
very frequently cupped his hands over his ears, then
removed them, as if he were exploring the role of the ear

in hearing. This activity, which produces a rush of sound like the roar of the ocean one hears when holding a conch shell to the ear, has two startling effects. One is a marked withdrawal of attention from the outer world and a centering of it on one's own body. The other is a feeling of pressure and fullness in the ear with a distinct sense of the body-rind as a demarcation between the outside and the inside. It seems as if the rush of sound were coming from inside the ear rather than outside, as we ordinarily hear sounds. After three weeks Billy stopped doing this, but began to put his finger deep into his mouth and after a brief while to withdraw it. This was followed by a third repetitive activity: a rapid up-and-down oscillation of his index finger very close to his eye, brushing against his eyelashes. The finger placed deep into the mouth elicits a gagging response and a feeling of nausea arising deep within the body; similarly, the rapid oscillation of the finger close to the eye produces a flickering effect and the sense that the visual locus is inside the body.

The effects Billy produced on himself have several important characteristics in common. All dramatically shift attention from its usual locus outside the body to one inside and produce a particularly sharp sense of the distinction between inside and outside. All produce the illusion that sensation essentially evoked outside the self (though by the self, acting on the self) comes from within the self. If a child in the midst of a struggle over separation (as were Billy and most children his age) is acutely aware of a deficiency, an emptiness, within the self and if he is aware of an inner longing that can be satisfied only by the mother, a figure located outside the self, then his experiments with his own body could have been an effort to master the sense of inner emptiness and depletion and the acute awareness that the nourishing center of his being was located outside the self. This sense and awareness are brought into sharp focus by the reactions to separation so common in children during their second year. Billy's autogenous behaviors were, however, unusual. The high level of object-loss anxiety he had to cope with led, we think, to a complementary greater-than-usual instability in the developing sense of self. His behavior was an effort to firm up the uncertain outline of the body image. In this connection we recall Bishop Berkeley's famous paradox about perception and psychic reality (cf., Fraser, 1871): The rose we gaze at is outside in the garden, but our perception of it involves processes within our bodies. This paradox is a real problem in the child's development of a sense of body self and is resolved only through varied and circuitous routes, some of which Billy demonstrated to us. We should stress how difficult it was for us to empathize quickly with Billy's repetitive games. For some time we felt sure the behavior was significant, but we were baffled by it. It was not until we tried out his actions on ourselves that we understood them.

During Billy's struggle with separation and self-definition, his mother left him, at age 16 months, in their own apartment in the care of his grandmother while she joined her husband on leave for two weeks. During this period, Billy continued to attend the nursery and there was very little observable change in his behavior, except that he seemed somewhat subdued and absolutely refused milk. He had previously taken many bottles of milk, usually when he awoke at night. His grandmother told us that he was eating solid foods well, perhaps even voraciously, which he had not done before his mother went away. When his mother returned, he immediately recognized her and expressed genuine pleasure at seeing her again. Except for the first 24 hours when he resumed drinking his milk, he continued to refuse it in spite of his mother's extraordinary efforts. She tried mixing the milk with chocolate syrup and with a variety of vegetable colorings until she hit upon a mixture of orange juice and milk—which he accepted, curds and all. In was some three months before he once again drank plain milk. With his mother's return, he ate even less solid food than he had before she left, and this continued throughout the remaining time he was with us. He refused milk for the next three months presumably because of anger at having been separated from her. We surmised that his anger was split off and externalized (Mahler, 1971) and the partial image of the bad mother projected onto the bottle of milk, which was then rejected.

Most children during their second year show very little alteration in their behavior while the parents are actually away, except for manifesting a sober and subdued mood, a reaction generally attributed to the child's focus on the mental representation of the object while mother is actually absent (McDevitt, 1975) in order to maintain an inner balance and integrity. But after the reunion, the full force of raging anger plays a large role in organizing the infant's behavior and responses.

Within a very few days after his mother's return,

Billy's separation reactions seemed to increase in intensity. He appeared chronically apprehensive and unhappy, and seemed little able to involve himself with things or people—children or adults. In contrast to his earlier pleasurable, babbling curiosity about everything in the nursery, now it was difficult for him to get interested in any sustained activity. Compared with the other children his age who were by now developing more or less elaborate symbolic play (see Chapter 5) and at times a surprisingly rich social involvement with adults and other children, Billy's development seemed quite impoverished in these respects.

Billy now kept an anxious eye on his mother in the nursery. If he lost sight of her or she left for even a brief period, he broke into an anxious, miserable sobbing and was inconsolable until reunited with her. At the end of the nursery sessions, he often burst into tears and attempted to follow a mother and child who were leaving, although he had shown no particular interest in that pair during the morning. During this period he developed a close relationship with the young woman who served as one of his observers. If she was already there when he came into the nursery in the morning, he insisted on being held in her arms for at least five minutes. He especially could not tolerate her departure from the nursery, even for brief periods. For some months, when hurt, he often went to her in preference to his mother. After about three months, when these acute separation reactions had largely diminished, Billy distinctly avoided this preferred closeness to his observer.

About a week after his mother's return, Billy was in the bathroom along with all the other children, playing with the toilet flush and seat cover and with the water. A group of observers had gathered outside the door to watch. One by one all the other children wandered out, leaving only Billy. Whereupon he crowded into a corner between the toilet and the wall and bent over slightly, touching his abdomen and pelvic area with his hands and gazing fixedly at the floor for about a minute or two. He then covered his eyes with his hands and squatted. This tense, almost manneristic withdrawal was highly disturbing to the adults, and the observer nearest him held her arms out to him. He cringed but then allowed himself to be picked up by his own observer. In this instance Billy's acute and profound withdrawal seemed to be a reaction to the large number of adults in close proximity observing him, an aspect of the resurgence of stranger anxiety following the separation.

We believe that with the separation reaction, enhanced by the two-week-long actual separation, Billy developed profound ambivalence which he dealt with in part by defensive splitting of the good and bad object representations (Mahler, 1971). This process had already been reflected in his refusal of his milk bottle and in the renewed sharp stranger anxiety; in both cases his anger toward his mother was projected onto external objects — the bottle and the unfamiliar adult — and dealt with by avoidance. His reaction to the adults in the bathroom incident probably resulted from the same process of splitting and projection. This need to withdraw repeatedly and to focus on the fantasy of closeness to mother reflected the serious inroads his ambivalence had made on his playful activity. His strong attachment to his own female observer suggests how much his relationship with his mother was marred by ambivalence.

Billy's reaction to separation was also shown by his response to noise. When he was 13 months old, he became moderately apprehensive when the doorbell buzzed or the television blared. This sensitivity to sound had not been noted earlier and first appeared while his mother was away. After his mother's return from her trip, he was extraordinarily sensitive to sound, whether or not his mother was present. Some sounds, even the doorbell in a neighbor's apartment, threw him into a paroxysm of apprehension. Most of the sounds that provoked an anxious reaction can roughly be characterized as loud and sudden. We can state with confidence that Billy's reaction to sound had been quite ordinary before. Along with this anxious sensitivity to all sound, Billy seemed to develop an unusual interest in and discrimination of distant and barely audible sounds. He would stop in the midst of the general din of the nursery, repeat a sound to himself, and be satisfied only when he could identify its source. These sounds— the hum of a neon bulb, the roar of a jet airplane, the whir of a cement mixer—not only were not heard by the adults in the room until Billy drew attention to them, but even then could often be identified only with difficulty and after utmost concentration.

This enhanced sensitivity to sound seems to result from a somatizaton of anxiety in the auditory sphere and may be related to the many fears of loud noises and other unusual sounds commonly encountered during the period of heightened stranger reaction at eight or nine months of age. For example, an infant boy of eight months, seen in another setting, would break into almost inconsolable paroxysms of screaming which, after considerable searching, we found was provoked by the high-pitched, barely audible sounds of a garbage truck or jet airplane. Just before the appearance of this sound sensitivity, the little boy had shown a very transitory stranger reaction that disappeared and seemed to be replaced by the anxious reaction to sound.

If we consider the external perceptual indications by means of which the infant builds his image of the mothering figure, it is clear that the tactile and kinesthetic modalities are sensors in close proximity and consequently are most immediate. The olfactory clues are intermediate; they permit some distance and may even linger after the object disappears. The visual and auditory spheres permit greater distance. Hearing cannot easily be focused in one direction or another and does not delineate the object so clearly. Furthermore, the auditory sphere stands alone in that it offers the slightest and most ephemeral sensory indication of the object, for the object may be heard in another room, giving no other sensory indication; this is not regularly true in any other perceptual sphere. Perhaps this is why anxiety is shown by auditory behavior in these two early normal crises of object relatedness—separation reaction and stranger reaction—as the infant tries to establish an internal representation of the object. Moreover, in adult analysis, memories of sounds in another room at night often evoke only a rather isolated though vivid association of an anxious feeling of loneliness and being left out. This is usually, and we believe correctly, interpreted as an early residue from the reaction to the primal scene. We suggest that the anxious involvement of the auditory sphere in the separation reaction may serve as an additional important determinant in such auditory memory residues from early childhood.

Finally, it seems probable that these considerations may illuminate hallucinatory phenomena in adult schizophrenic patients. At times the psychotic ego is flooded with unneutralized aggression, and, concomitant with regression, a deterioration occurs in self and object representations. Many ego functions, such as the sharp delineation of inside-outside, deteriorate and introjective-projective mechanisms become prominent. We propose that the ensuing object-loss anxiety and fears of dissolution of the self may evoke the primitive mechanism we have described in these infants: the anxiety becomes manifested in the auditory sphere, in hallucinations of sound. We speculate that in the separation reactions and stranger reactions of normal children the resultant implicit strain in the relation with the object evokes a disruptive amount of aggression which is dealt with by this primitive forerunner of defense — the somatization of aggression in the auditory sphere.

A contributing factor in Billy's relatively marked separation reaction may be that his mother, with her husband away for an entire year, suffered from loneliness and consequently became too close to her little boy; she may have resisted his maturing tendency to grow away from her. We have already referred to the importance of the father in the whole process of separation-individuation (see Chapter 1). Furthermore, the father's actual disappearance would increase the infant's apprehension about the mother's possible disappearance as well.

At 14 months, when his separation reactions had been clearly established for several weeks, Billy showed increasing interest in his genitals. Until this time, both our own observations and his mother's reports showed that Billy handled his genitals only casually and infrequently during changes of diaper and in his bath. But from 14 months through the remainder of the time we followed him, observations and reports confirmed that at virtually all changes of diaper and during baths he handled his penis, squeezing and pulling it, in a concentrated and persistent fashion.

When Billy was between 15 and 16 months old, his mother several times reported that he would, with a concentrated expression, clutch his penis for a minute or two, his whole face would flush, and he would strain as if with a bowel movement. This behavior, which was observed over a two-to-three-week period only, suggests how indistinctly differentiated the genital sensation is from the anal, at least early in development.

For the four months following the separation experience, from 16 to 20 months, Billy's masturbation became more organized and had a more driven quality than previously. On a number of occasions both in the nursery and at home he was observed to lie prone on a ball or with some other toy tucked underneath his genital area and rock back and forth in a concentrated and withdrawn manner. This preferred masturbatory posture seemed to be a more erotized elaboration of the behavior pattern that developed following the bathroom experience, when he demonstrated a tense manneristic withdrawal. It will be recalled that following this experience he was frequently observed in the nursery to interrupt his activity and lie prone on the floor for a period of time in a withdrawn, dreamy state.

On a number of occasions during this same period, Billy straddled his mother's leg and vigorously rubbed himself back and forth. She seemed largely oblivious to the masturbatory meaning of this activity, explaining that he liked to play rocking horse on her leg. However, she was alarmed when on one occasion while she was changing a diaper and applying lotion to the whole perineal area, Billy took hold of her hand and placed it directly on his penis. On still another occasion, while his mother was playing with him and tickling him under his arms and chin, he took her hand, placed it on his penis, and began to rock back and forth in a state of obvious arousal.

At 15 months, after the early genital zone arousal had been firmly established and he had had several opportunities to observe his mother's genitals when he was in the bathroom while she used the toilet, Billy developed a sharp but circumscribed castration reaction. We noted a new uneasiness with broken toys and crayons and a new general body hypochondria. He reacted with anxiety to minor cuts and bruises, which a short while before he hardly seemed to notice, and on several occasions anxiously pointed to a "boo-boo" where none existed.

Billy's castration reaction was conspicuously different from the early castration reactions in the other boys we studied. All but four of the boys in our sample reacted to observing the anatomical difference by periods of denying it, by masturbating more often and more vigorously at times, by an increase in motor activity, and by beginning to turn to the father in identification. Not only did Billy have to cope with an instability in the basic self and object representations that was greater than usual, but he was unable to mobilize a defensive denial of the anatomical difference between the sexes supported by a growing identification with the father, since his father was absent.

At this same time Billy developed an interesting obligatory ritual on going to sleep which persisted throughout the ensuing months that he continued to attend the nursery. He had for seven or eight months been put down in his crib with a bottle and would fall asleep sometime after taking it. At around 15 months his mother found that after he drank from the bottle he would lie down prone and fall asleep with the bottle pressed against his penis. On those nights when his sleep was restless and he moved about in his crib a great deal so that he was no longer lying on the bottle pressed against his penis, he would wake up screaming. The choice of the bottle, an object so closely identified with the mother as a fetishistic defense against castration concerns, probably reflects the unusual prominence in Billy of object-loss and body-dissolution anxieties. It is significant for Billy's subsequent development that his masturbatory pattern increasingly took on the form of the going-to-sleep ritual, with all that this suggests about the invasion of his sexuality by defensive elements. During this same period we noted both from our own observations and the mother's reports that on a number of occasions Billy would clutch his penis when he was frustrated in an activity or angry with his mother, behavior that became more prominent in his

16th and 17th months when he was at the height of his separation reaction following the mother's two-week absence.

Ordinarily the genital and anal zones may serve the infant as body channels for the expression of the normal transitory splitting of the primary ambivalence, a defense that aids in the gradual consolidation of the basic self and object representations. However, with the emergence of Billy's severe preoedipal castration reaction, the hostile aspect of his primary ambivalence was intensified. The increase in hostility led to an erotization of aggression, an abnormal development which became even more prominent after the two-week separation from his mother. We believe it was this erotization of aggression, reflected in his clutching his penis, that gave his masturbation its unusually sharp and driven quality. This trend served to further mar his developing object relatedness.

Billy's severe castration problem left in its wake a significant erotization of aggression, the basis for a sado-masochistic object relationship, and a masturbatory pattern which had taken on a much more focally defensive character than is normally the case. We have indicated that, although his castration reaction had been a severe one, it was at the same time very circumscribed. Although he showed the usual defensive displacement of castration concerns — the general body hypochrondria and intolerance of broken objects — all in the service of denial, he failed to demonstrate the significant elaboration of denial in symbolic fantasy, which usually emerges in developing preoedipal castration reactions. In fact, Billy seemed to show an inhibition of symbolic fan-

tasy development not only around his castration problem but in his general activity and play. We believe his
defensive pattern was expressed in a firm, concrete form
in his attachment to the bottle as part of the going-to-
sleep ritual which, through its crystallization, tended to
constrict his further development, with a resultant inhibition in the emergence of symbolic fantasy.

Although we were unable to follow the details of
his development further, reports that we have received
suggest that at age five years Billy not only continued to
be profoundly intolerant of being left by his parents,
but also reacted with anxiety when friends of his parents
who were relatively strange to him left the house or
were seen off at the railroad station.

CHAPTER 5

THE SYMBOLIC FUNCTION

Play, that ubiquitous and unique form of childhood behavior, has been studied extensively by representatives
of a variety of disciplines, including psychoanalysis and
psychology. Considerations of the content of play as
well as of its function have been prominent in the
writings of Freud (1900, 1920), Waelder (1932), Erikson (1950), Peller (1954), and many others. Another
aspect of play, its inherent or underlying mental organization or structure, has received less attention and may
be particularly important with regard to the nature and
genesis of thought, especially in connection with the development of the symbolic function.

Whereas many consider the symbolic function the
hallmark of man's evolutionary achievement, the
genesis of this function in its earliest form of play has
received relatively little attention, although it is precisely this early form which may influence the character
of the symbolic function in a definitive way.

Our interest in the symbolic function stems from the fact that the capacity for verbalization, an advanced form of symbolization, is only slowly expanding during the second year when the capacity for play has already achieved considerable complexity. It is true that the underlying psychological meaning to the infant of much, if not most, of his behavior during the first year or so of life is the most difficult to verify, according to commonly accepted criteria of scientific validity. Nonetheless, the study of play seems to offer a promising window through which we might be able to view the effect of the progressive stages of psychosexual and object relations development upon concurrently developing mental or cognitive processes. How do the somatic and social experiences of the second year of life affect the infant's capacity to deal with his own body, with other people, and with the inanimate world? What are the modifying effects of the psychosexual zonal experiences upon this particular aspect of cognition, the symbolic function?

An early reflection of mental life is found in a group of behaviors that first appear as very primitive actions, typical instances of which are the shaking of a rattle, the mouthing of a ring, or the squeezing of a toy. This aspect of mentation, commonly known as "play," ranges from these simple expressions of impulses as actions to extremely complex series of behaviors which have developed by the end of the second year and from which inferences can be drawn concerning the nature of the underlying mental process. While the very early and primitive forms of play probably represent the direct expression of an impulse without modulation in any aspect of that impulse, such transformations are soon evident. These transformational processes are extremely varied. They include displacement to another body discharge pathway (kicking with the feet rather than squeezing with the hand), interposition of a part of the self (biting one's own finger rather than a toy), interposition of another person (squeezing the mother's arm rather than the toy), and a wide assortment of other modifications whereby the impulse to act has been modulated to some degree by means of a substitution. These substitutions constitute the somatic basis for the symbolic function, whether the modified impulses derive primarily from instinctual (or biological) sources or are more distinctly motivated by the incipient human attachments. Eventually, through an ever-more-complex series of such substitutions, the symbolic systems of thought and language are finally attained.

One of the earliest descriptions of the symbolic equation of one organ with another was offered by Ferenczi (1913), when he described how one part of the body might be equated with another, one subsequently replacing the other. Following repression of the masturbatory impulses, overemphasis of the upper part of the body in general came about as the result of displacement from below upward. Greenacre (1954) elaborated on this theme of the early plasticity of body experiences when she described somatic configurations or patterns of behavior that arose through particularly strong or repetitive stimulation, somatic patterns that would then be substituted for one another under conditions of stress.

Studying the symbolic function from an entirely

different viewpoint, Piaget (1923, 1936, 1937, 1945) observed the play of normal infants and derived from these observations his theory of mental functioning underlying this play. Piaget was interested in its role in the development of cognition. His theory of sensorimotor intelligence views action and ideation as different aspects of a continuum, the earliest forms of thought being the sensorimotor actions themselves. Gradually these action patterns achieve mental representation of such reliability that the child can intentionally rearrange them in thought, without any manifest action at all. Problem-solving now takes place at a far more advanced stage in symbolic functioning. This usually begins somewhere between 16 to 18 months of age and constitutes a qualitatively different form of mentation, which Piaget has identified as the hallmark of his Stage VI of sensorimotor development. Piaget has provided detailed descriptions of the line of progression from the earliest forms of partially semisymbolic play to those forms of play in which the symbolism has become far more abstract in quality.

The following listing of various kinds of play observed in our nursery has been categorized according to the degree of concreteness as well as the complexity that characterized these play sequences, utilizing Piaget's developmental progression with regard to play symbolism.

(1) Play consisting of simple direct action on animate or inanimate objects (the substitution of one behavior for another cannot be inferred from the overt act itself): banging, pulling, pushing, shaking, turning objects, piling objects, etc.

(2) Early semisymbolic play, which includes the use of a concrete object, whether animate or inanimate, for the reproduction of an action the infant has already experienced. For example, the infant places a doll in a toy bed and covers it with a blanket, "feeds" it with a toy bottle filled with water, places it on a toy chair, or undresses it and places it on a toy toilet (the beginning of "pretend play" is evident here, although the concrete props — the doll, the blanket, the water-filled bottle, etc. — are necessary components of these early semisymbolic forms of play).

(3) More advanced forms of semisymbolic play: these play sequences are more abstract in that the actual concrete props are less necessary, i.e., the child holds the doll up and pretends to feed it with a bottle, although no bottle is actually present; or puts the doll to sleep in an imaginary bed on the floor.

The early forms of semisymbolic games serve the purpose of rethinking and modifying the impact of experiences in the only manner available to infants of this age — that is, through body action. As the symbolic function continues to develop, body action is projected onto objects in the outer world, which begin to stand for other objects. In the more primitive forms of semisymbolic play, the inanimate object chosen for representation resembles the original version in close and even exact detail. Thus, the young infant of 18 months or so requires that his "play" bed actually resemble a real bed in its shape and form, although indeed it may be smaller in its dimensions. By the time the toddler reaches the third year, however, a folding chair or other surface may serve as a bed for the doll, since his imagination now supplies the bedlike qualities. A more complex level of symbolism has been attained in that the signifier does not have to share as many qualities of what it signifies in order to sustain its symbolic meaning for the child. In this sense, the word is, of course, the most abstract form of symbolism since it shares no attributes at all with what it signifies.

The earliest words are, of course, only partially abstract in the sense that "boy" means the "boy next door" or the "boy in the book whose name is Jim" but does not yet signify all boys everywhere. These early boy/girl labels, like other early words, are quite unstable during the second year and therefore their use hardly constitutes evidence that the child has developed a firm conviction that there are two sexes, or what the attributes of these two sexes might be. We cannot agree, therefore, with those who believe that the use of the label "boy" or "girl" testifies to the child's sense of his own sexual identity.

Piaget's studies of play as early symbolic forms led to his theoretical position that the symbolic system of language develops along a separate line from that of play. He noted that the word, the symbolic basis of language, is assigned an arbitrary and conventional meaning, one that evolves from the environment. In contrast to the word, the play symbol may be and, in fact, usually is assigned an individual or egocentric meaning by the child, a meaning that continues long after language is developed. Piaget believes that there are important differences between the two symbolic systems of language and play precisely because the word has an arbitrary and conventionally assigned meaning, one that involves a social relationship between the child and his environment, whereas the play symbol is not modified by social experience to the same degree and can be retained in its original form.

In contrast to the symbolic system of language, then, Piaget regards the play or "ludic" symbol as the product of individual thought. Not until the age of eight or nine years, according to Piaget, does this play finally become "accommodated" to reality, tending to reproduce it. Piaget believes that dream symbolism is but a continuation of symbolic play, that the unconscious symbolism of psychoanalysis is a particular case of symbolism in general, and that much of the conscious symbolism of adults experienced as visual or other forms of imagery is related developmentally to unconscious symbolism.

In summary, Piaget believes that the symbolic function has two separate lines of development, both stemming from its earliest form in play. One line proceeds toward language while the other continues as the nonverbal symbolism of dreams, metaphors, and other types of imagery.

The issue of whether the symbolic function develops along two separate lines has been of considerable interest to us as we have tried to trace the influence of early psychosexual experiences on various aspects of the personality, including the cognitive area.

Not only play patterns in general, but also early genital self-stimulation patterns show differences that are consistent for boys as a group and for girls as a group. These patterns undoubtedly reflect underlying psychological differences between the sexes which may be partly genetic and partly cultural in origin. Erikson's (1950) concept of instinctual modes of play behavior has provided a helpful framework for deciphering the meaning of much of the play behavior we observed. Erikson suggested that the configurational or space-organizing properties that characterize these modes are derived from body functions, and that these later become styles of thought and social interaction.

Werner and Kaplan (1963) have extended Erikson's original theoretical models, analyzing patterns of early sensorimotor functions according to their vectorial properties—properties that can be extended to later-developing forms of thought. Such qualities as direction, force, balance, rhythm, and enclosingness are useful in identifying the dynamic similarities which are experienced by the infant in relation to different body parts. Thus, the fingers shape and snap as the mouth does, providing the infant with an early basis of experience in such dynamic similarities between entities — body parts in this instance — which are thenceforth linked and may substitute for one another. Such substitution provides one pathway for the formation of symbols.

By utilizing Erikson's and Werner and Kaplan's structural concepts of patterns and modes of functioning, we have been able to identity infant behavior patterns that are highly relevant to the issue of the impact of psychosexual development upon the rest of personality development. The clinical material presented later in this chapter provides many instances of how the influence of zonal experiences (oral, anal, urinary, and genital) could be clearly identified through the clusters and patterns of play that emerged simultaneously with the specific zone arousal. For example, at about the time of emergence of anal-zone awareness, usually between 12 and 15 months of age, semisymbolic play patterns repetitively seemed to reflect the anal influence; these included interest in the toilet flush and bowl, emptying and filling games, scattering and piling games, smearing, and interest in "peg" games (in which the peg is pushed through an opening and then retrieved from below), and in the anal function itself.

As urinary awareness emerged a few months later, sometime between 14 and 16 months in most of our research group, the infants became fascinated with their own urinary stream and with the urination of parents, peers, and animals as well—that is, the urinary zone itself. But they were also now fascinated by repetitive play with faucets, hoses, watering cans, and many other types of pouring or "urinary" types of play. In this manner, the connection between the experience of sensations of the anal and urinary zones could be clearly identified in their projection onto both other people and the inanimate world.

With the emergence in our infants of urinary and then genital awareness, Erikson's (1950) descriptions of the sex differences in block play were amply confirmed as we recorded that girls were now building largely enclosed structures while boys began to pile tall towers as a projection onto the inanimate world of the sense of their own genital body image. Furthermore, a great variety of thrusting, jabbing, and throwing games of a phallic quality now occupied the boys in great part, while the girls became more and more absorbed in doll play and nurturing activities.

Although we have not studied language development in detail, data relating to the language area were collected. The play sequences between 16 and 19 months were often accompanied by vocalizations of various kinds, but not by verbalization to the outside world in most instances. And when verbalization did occur, it often seemed to be self-directed rather than meant as a communication to others. These findings concur with Vigotsky's (1934) concept of "inner speech," i.e., thinking for oneself in contrast to "external speech," which is addressed to the outer world. (Vigotsky described this inner speech as "thinking in pure meaning," more like a dynamic fluttering between word and thought, without unitary and separate structures and difficult to articulate because of its inconsistent tie to words.)

Langer (1942), discussing nonverbal thought in relation to the nature and development of symbolism in musical and visual artistic forms, calls these forms "presentational" symbolism, in that the meaning of each symbolic element can be understood only through the meaning of the whole and through its relations within the total structure. Finally, Vigotsky's and Langer's nonverbal symbolic systems share two additional features of particular interest; the lack of negation and the use of symbols that do not have a fixed meaning, features seen in the early semisymbolic play described by Piaget as well as in primary-process thinking.

It seems likely that play of this particular type reflects underlying primary-process thinking as it flourishes under the impact of psychosexual and object relations developmental pressures of the second year of life, providing some means for modulating and modifying these pressures, yet also shaped by these pressures. Perhaps it is the uniquely open-ended semisymbolic nature of this play, derivative of the various zonal and object-relations experiences of this specific age, which later provides the basis for the symbolism of dreams and other nonverbal symbolic forms, as Piaget has suggested.

Our incidental data in the area of language development are also in accord with an aspect of Bruner's (1974, 1977) theory of language acquisition. Based upon studies of reciprocal play between mothers and infants, rather than solitary play, Bruner has traced reciprocal games as they develop from early joint "tasks" ordinarily carried out in conventional ways which are agreed upon by each mother-child pair. This mutual agreement may be even more important, in Bruner's view, than the actual performance of the particular act. The ambience of play is a necessary ingredient for these interactions, providing a tension-free, flexible, and creative opportunity for the infant to practice different ways of dealing with the social and physical environment. This playful atmosphere offers the child the opportunity of mastering rules and conventions governing behavior between the two members of the dyad.

In contrast to older views of language acquisition, Bruner thinks that language does not grow out of need for drive satisfaction primarily, or the need for alleviation of other physical distress. Indeed, an excessive degree of such pressure would, in Bruner's view, interfere with language development. The prespeech communicative acts between mother and child provide the precursors of grammatical competence and constitute the first advance in symbolic development leading toward speech.

Our data appear to confirm Bruner's findings of an increasing complexity of reciprocal playful interactions where there is an absence of an acute need state and the mother is playfully attentive.

It should be emphasized that the reciprocal playful mother-child interactions Bruner describes are not identical with Piaget's semisymbolic play. The latter usually occurs when the child is playing alone, and it does not involve the mother's participation. Piaget assumes that the child expresses his past experiences as well as his current needs through the semisymbolic play he studied, a conclusion our own data tend to confirm. In those children whose development was proceeding smoothly, the type of semisymbolic games Piaget described emerged at the appropriate ages he predicted. In addition to these, many forms of reciprocal play interaction between mother and child appeared and continued to increase in complexity.

However, a number of infants in our sample suffered from delays and distortions in both the play and language areas of symbolic functioning—infants who developed the most severe preoedipal castration reactions at the time of the emergence of the early genital phase. These disturbances in symbolic development took many forms. Several girls who developed language unusually early seemed to utilize this capacity more as a defense against their fears and anxiety than for the expression of thought in general. Several other girls and

two of the boys who suffered severe preoedipal castration reactions became preoccupied with repetitive and
rather stereotyped forms of play in which the central
theme consisted of the search for the missing phallus—
in the case of the girls, on their mothers, other females,
and dolls; in the boys, on themselves. This "genital-
derivative" play, as we have called it, consisted of placing a rod or pencil or other phallic-shaped concrete object in the approximate vicinity of the missing phallus.

A number of girls and one of the boys who suffered
from severe castration reactions developed a temporary
regression in their language, in that they avoided using
the male pronoun entirely for some time—often for periods lasting several weeks or even months.

Many of the girls with more moderate reactions
showed a strong interest in yet another form of symbolic
function during the preoedipal castration reaction:
drawing and other forms of graphic representation.

Finally, most of the girls and three of the boys who
suffered severe castration reactions became attached to
a series of concrete objects, many of which were actually phallic in shape. These phallic replacements are yet
another aspect of the many facets of the symbolic function that are affected by experiences related to the
emerging sense of genital identity during the second half
of the second year.

Rose

The girl whose development we describe here
showed a peculiar and unusually early use of concrete
objects in a symbolic way during the course of her second year. Although these did not constitute her entire

symbolic repertoire, they were by far her favorites, and differed from those usually seen in young children of this age in that their use persisted well beyond the average age and was particularly intense and often obligatory for her comfort. Furthermore, her parents seem to have participated to an unusual degree in her choice of these objects.

Rose, a first-born child, had shared the parental bedroom during her first six months of life. She had suffered from fairly severe early colic and had worn an orthopedic brace on both legs from about six weeks to five months of age because of a mild malalignment of both feet. Each evening her father removed the braces in preparation for her bath, which he always administered. At four or five months of age, concurrently with the onset of stranger anxiety, Rose developed a "look" consisting of partially lowered eyelids from beneath which she peered in rapid darting sequences. Her parents called it her "flirtatious" or "coy" look and said it was reserved for men only. Rose was also more than ordinarily devoted to her father, a fact noted by her mother when we first came to know Rose when she was 13 months old.

At 12 months of age, Rose began to finger her external genitals during her diapering. Although this was more frequent and intense than the casual, fleeting exploratory genital touching which, according to our observations, is characteristic of the genital exploration at the end of the first year, it was still relatively low-pitched.

At 15½ months of age, Rose had just begun unaided locomotion, a mild delay for which the braces were held partially responsible. This coincided with her mother's first trimester of pregnancy, a circumstance which was to prove significant for Rose's future development. At about the same time, she began to indicate the stool in her diaper by both gesture and word, and her general behavior was characterized by her parents as quite negative. She had frequently witnessed a male playmate's urination, but was not allowed to see her father urinate until her 16th month, when she clamored so vehemently that her mother persuaded him to permit it. She reacted initially with fascination and intense excitement. Shortly thereafter, she pointed to the water faucet, using her word for urination, a displacement her mother encouraged and which was continued by the infant in the form of water play later on. However, she consistently resisted her mother's mild attempts to train her for urination.

Rose's interest in the sight of her father's penis and urination and her devotion to him in general continued unabated. She also pursued and flirted with a number of male observers in the nursery, often insisting upon sitting on their laps and "riding" their crossed ankles. There was no doubt about her clear preference for males.

Her genital manipulation, which now included fingering and stroking of the labia and the clitoral area while she was being diapered, was no longer the relatively calm affair of her 12th month. It was accompanied by giggling and a facial expression of inner absorption.

At 17 months, a series of new behaviors heralded the onset of an early castration reaction. One day in the nursery, Rose stood with both legs spread apart as a stream of urine trickled down her inner thighs alongside her diaper. Her facial expression was described by three observers as bewildered, upset, and embarrassed; as she took a step toward her mother, she looked back at the puddle of urine and then called for her mother's assistance. She seemed to be ashamed — perhaps a reflection of her awareness of the genital difference. She now resisted diaper changes regularly; her mother reported mild stool retention, and Rose pointed to nonexistent "boo-boo's" on her fingers. She developed a sleep disturbance, was afraid to sit down in the bathtub, and consistently avoided looking at the penis of her male playmate, pointing to his umbilicus instead. (We interpret this as a displacement upward, a defense we have seen quite frequently in similar situations.) Her previously active masturbation declined markedly.

The background of Rose's earlier experiences provides a clue to this new development of a castration reaction. We think that the unusually erotic nature of her early contact with her father for her first six months had contributed to a somewhat excessive and premature genital arousal. In addition, she was later repeatedly exposed to the sight of her father's penis when he urinated. Greenacre (1953b), referring to such genital exposures, states that the awareness of the genital difference "becomes painful and the subject of envy, especially if the child has recently been subjected to other narcissistic blows and deprivations (such as illness, separation from the mother, loss of a playmate) and that a sense of being at a disadvantage with envy of the *richer* boy emerges then in a situation of special vulnerability" (pp. 32–33).

We believe that her mother's pregnancy had constituted just such deprivation for Rose. The gradual withdrawal of the mother's interest threatened the infant's already wavering self-esteem and body-image stability. Her avoidance of looking at other children's penises and the decreased masturbation constituted behavioral evidence of her psychological state of envy, while her earlier fears of body disintegration and object loss were rekindled. We saw her anxiety about diaper changes and urinary loss and her sleep disturbance as behavioral evidence of these earlier concerns.

Prior to the events described, Rose had never been interested in dolls. As her phallic-urinary preoccupation and her stool retention continued, she developed an attachment to several dolls, and insisted that three of them accompany her to bed. At the same time she was no longer interested in her pacifier and blanket. She now used words for "mother" and for the act of separation for the first time. Rose had evidently attained a new level of development in the use of both concrete and verbal symbols.

Soon a whole series of additional concrete symbols developed. Rose searched the inner coat pockets of her father and other males, consistently selecting the pen from among other objects she found there. Cigars and wristwatches were similarly sought. These three groups of objects, all of which were particularly important to her father, seemed now to have been endowed with the excitement formerly observed when she saw his penis.

From the 18th to the 19th month on, Rose and her mother became locked in an oppositional struggle. While Rose's exploration of her own body ceased, she threw inanimate objects or held on to them with ferocious tenacity. Her mother, who responded by using every distraction she could devise, complained of loneliness and hoped her next child would be a boy. We think that she intuitively sensed the struggle in which Rose was engaged.

After a month of consistently avoiding the genital and anal area, Rose returned to visual and tactile exploration with new intensity at 19 months. (This pattern of repeated emergence and disappearance of behaviors, which indicates an underlying area of conflict, is characteristic of the second year of life.) In relation to her own body, her hands intruded beneath her wet and soiled diapers, and she resumed her masturbation during diapering with prolonged clitoral squeezing and rubbing, followed by pressing her thighs together as she searched the room until her gaze found her favorite male observer. She also turned her attention again to her mother's body and investigated her umbilicus. Dolls, too, were searched as she lifted their dresses and pointed at and named umbilicus, breasts, and genitals.

The upsurge of all this body exploration was accompanied by the appearance of a new crop of concrete symbolic objects. It seemed that her search for the phallus had widened from exploration of her own body into the outer world. She collected crayons and chalk, in addition to the ever-present pens, all of which shared the structural (vectorial, configurational) aspect of the father's penis.

Shortly, she began to take toys with her secretly whenever she left home or the nursery, often in a rather sly way, perhaps an early form of "kleptomania." (Her mother's increasingly obvious pregnancy and Rose's search for the missing phallus probably played their parts in the genesis of this symptom.) That the somewhat secretive "stealing" was accompanied by evidence of early superego development was clear from the "no-no" with which Rose chided herself as she proceeded to carry out a forbidden act.

By 20 months, Rose had reached a climax of possessiveness in relation to an assortment of concrete objects: toy cars; the tops of pens, which she hid in closets; crayons, with which she marked walls; and a toy wristwatch, which she regularly lost and found again. Finally, she placed one of the crayons between her labia during a diapering in an all-too-vivid demonstration of the source of her distress and the symbolic significance of her interest in crayons.

We believe that the mother's advancing pregnancy gave a particularly strong impetus to Rose's dilemma as she grappled with the problem of penis envy. During the 22nd month, Rose seemed absorbed both in her struggle to understand the inside-outside aspect of the anal zone itself and in her search for the anal phallus. She explored her anus with her fingers, insisted upon being diapered "from the rear," and was distressed at removal of her soiled diapers. Awareness of anal functioning and the search for the anal phallus were externalized in her extensive play with boxes as she explored their inside-outside dimensions. She hoarded a multitude of "possessions," but was especially devoted to her picture puzzles and her supply of pennies. One night, when she finally had a stool in her toidy, having acceded to her mother's wishes, she looked bewildered and confused as she identified it by her parents' word for bowel movement.

Her anger at her mother was quite evident. The increase in hostile aggression now threatened the already marred mother-child relationship, and this new conflict seemed to result in the development of new defenses. A new devotion to neatness accompanied new fears of loud noises and of going down the slide, indicating that her angry wishes and her fear of loss of control had been externalized and displaced.

Then the oral zone became involved as an additional site of inside-outside activities, and many regressive oral activities appeared. She bit people, mouthed her mother's buttons, and once again requested her previously abandoned pacifier and bottle. Her diet became remarkably restricted to slices of cucumbers, carrots, and other similarly shaped solids. The incorporative fantasy motivating these behaviors was clearly revealed when she removed the pen from her male observer's pocket (calling him "Daddy" as she did so), placed the pen in her mouth, and said "Pee-pee."

Rose's mother had always offered diversion rather than direct frustration in her interaction with her child. She was remarkably clever at this and had rarely resorted to a direct confrontation of wills. Now, as she tried to help Rose in her continuing distress over the loss of the "stool-phallus," she demonstrated the route followed by the stool in the soiled "Pamper" as it was emptied into the toilet or placed in the garbage chute and thence removed by the garbage truck. In so doing, the mother offered a route for symbolic displacement with which Rose immediately complied. She became a devoted follower of garbage trucks, which she identified even at great distances. That her mother's unspoken disapproval of the anal exploration had been understood was evident as Rose began to hide from her mother during defecation. Her forbidden anal touching was externalized to constant and repetitive touching of garbage cans as well as the soil of potted plants and flowers and bushes.

Yet, in spite of such extensive use of externalization, her anger at her mother and other females emerged again and again. She bit, defied, and provoked her mother, as well as female nursery observers, while her "love affair" with her father and other males continued. She sought every opportunity to be with her father in the bathroom, built high towers, which she labeled "Daddies," for and with him, flirted vigorously with male observers, and appropriated their pens whenever she could. She built only horizontal structures when playing with her mother. And, as might be expected, her masturbation returned once again as she placed three fingers deeply within the vaginal introitus while being diapered. Whereas previously she had masturbated without any trace of self-consciousness, she now seemed aware of her mother's and a female observer's attention, and shifted her own gaze as if to avoid theirs. Some element of discomfort seemed to have become connected with her sexual activity.

When Rose's father was away from home for several days, many of her "lost and found" games reflected her feeling of loss. These included repetitive toilet flushing, shutting herself into boxes and rooms, piling blocks into containers, devotion to the old wristwatch, and a renewed "kleptomania" as she came and went from home to nursery. She also "stored" pennies in her mouth and explored every staircase. We speculate that once again these openings and enclosures represented the oral and anal routes she had earlier explored in her investigations of the oral and anal areas in search of the hidden stool-phallus. Now, in the absence of her father, she returned to these sites.

The father's homecoming gift for Rose was a replica of a New York garbage truck, which became her favorite toy, soon to be joined by a fire engine with expanding ladder, a jet plane, a car with battery-operated lights, and a gum machine operated by pushing a lever. The combined phallic and anal aspects of these toys (as well as their having been supplied by father) made them exquisitely appropriate for use as concrete symbols for the anal phallus she sought. Verbal confirmation for the stool-phallus equation came when she pointed to the genitalia of an anatomically correct male doll and used her word for bowel movement.

Toward the end of her mother's pregnancy, Rose positioned a flute at her genitals as she fell off to sleep one afternoon. She repeatedly tried to imitate a boy playmate's urination. She also arched her back in a comical and pathetic imitation of her mother's protruding abdomen. The threat of her mother's impending departure led to a new flurry of "hiding" games as well as tenacious clinging to her favorite toys.

Her sister was born just two weeks before Rose's second birthday. On the baby's first day at home, Rose urinated on the floor and on a bed near the woman who had cared for her during the mother's absence in what seemed to be an exquisite indication of the site of her distress as well as the cause of her anger.

We learned of her interest in two new objects which seemed to have symbolic significance. She received a small umbrella as a gift during her mother's absence — these parents sensed the cause of her discomfort all too keenly. The umbrella became an obligatory companion for a time; she took it to bed with her, named it in her sleep, pointed out pictures of umbrellas in books, and identified in dress material a tiny umbrella which was extremely difficult for others to see, even when pointed out. Its phallic shape, its connection with wetness, and its expandability made the umbrella a perfect phallic-urinary symbol. The other new symbolic object was a nipple shield her mother used for nursing. Rose placed this at her genital area repeatedly, reflecting the formation of the nipple-penis equation.

As her active interest in watching her father's urination dwindled, Rose demanded pens more than ever and began to show a new interest in drawing. This was combined with a new level of verbal achievement. The nonverbal and verbal attainments suggested that Rose had arrived at a new level of symbolic organization. We thought that the act of drawing, which incorporated the symbolic as well as the concrete use of a pen, might conceivably serve her as a future route for sublimation.

Two opportunities arose that afforded us some knowledge of Rose's subsequent development. In the first quarter of her third year she was strongly identified with her father's activities and had not yet resolved her conflict with her mother with regard to bowel training. By the time Rose was eight years old her attachment to her father was being somewhat diluted by her admiration for her current schoolteacher. She was a shy girl who did not have many friends but was quite talented in writing stories. Her teacher thought she might someday become a truly creative writer.

We have described the development of a group of concrete symbols which, we suggest, emerged under the influence of certain earlier body experiences, the particularly erotic father-child relationship and the thrust of anal, urinary, and genital awareness during the second half of the second year.

We agree with Greenacre (1956) that, while the oral, anal, and genital psychosexual zones ordinarily become active in a maturational sequence, a particular zone may be prematurely or excessively stimulated and called into ascendancy unusually early by a variety of experiences.

Rose showed just such an unusually early emergence of genital excitation and awareness. Her early gastric distress and the motor inhibition imposed by the orthopedic appliances had interfered with her body-image development, and the unusually erotic tie to the father had resulted in very early genital excitation with visual erotization (the flirtatious look) and masturbation of an intensity greater than is expected by 12 months of age. Then came her sharp awareness of the genital difference and her unusual distress over it.

As she entered the anal, urinary, and early genital phases, the search for the missing phallus began. Her tendency to use introjection and projection and visual incorporation, probably intensified by the erotic nature of her relation to her father, resulted in the adoption of concrete symbols — pens, crayons, cigars — rather than allowing her to turn to more abstract forms of symbolic expression. All of these concrete representations were similar in structure to her father's longed-for phallus and objects that he used consistently in his daily life. Thus, we have association by structural *pars pro toto* thinking and by contiguity with the loved object.

Rose then sought for a phallus at the anal zone. We noted the same tendency to deal with her anxiety about the reawakened fears of body disintegration and anal loss through the use of a variety of concrete objects or symbols — the garbage truck, gum machine, pennies, and so on. Finally, the flute, the umbrella, and the nipple shield were used during the painful phase of her displacement by the new baby, and the disappearance of her mother's phalliclike protruding abdomen. It seemed that the underlying body-image instability required additional bolstering, a need met through her intensive use of concrete objects. Such a development would appear to constitute a distortion of the symbolic function.

It is of interest that Rose used dolls only during the period of peak anxiety about the genital difference, in a flurry of identification with her mother and the new baby, and then abandoned them permanently. We speculate that her identification with her mother was seriously disrupted precisely in relation to that aspect of femininity connected with childbearing. For it was the birth of Rose's sister that precipitated the most severe hostile accretion to her already ambivalent relationship with her mother.

Rose's choice of early concrete symbols was characterized by a limited range, more rigid adherence to a particular type of pattern or structure in the symbols chosen, and an obligatory quality. In addition, they were objects which had been especially invested by mother or father. Usually, these early concrete symbols are given up. Some may gradually go into hiding, perhaps to develop into the hidden fetishes of women described by Greenacre (1960). It is possible that such a persistent and special attachment to concrete symbols will affect the later form of the symbolic function, accentuating its development toward a nonverbal or primary-process type of thinking rather than a fuller expression of thought and affect by means of language itself.

Play is an activity that is not only pleasurable but also provides an opportunity to re-experience in a controlled way those situations which may have aroused anxiety in the infant. Beyond these two functions lies a vast area of growing symbolic complexity with regard to the expression of psychological states, ideas, fantasies, and other forms of mental functioning.

CHAPTER 6

CONGENITAL DEFECT AND
THE EARLY GENITAL PHASE

One of the conditions originally postulated to produce a
severe preoedipal castration reaction was the existence
of a major congenital defect. In this chapter we describe
the development of Ruth, whose congenital defect required that she wear a small pillow between her diaper
and perineal area from her third to 12th month in order
to correct the hip dislocation with which she was born.
The defect also required repeated medical examinations
during her first year. The resulting early disturbance in
achieving a relatively stable concept of her body and in
the developing relationship with her mother distorted
and delayed the separation-individuation process and
interfered with the establishment of an optimally stable
maternal mental representation.

RUTH
Developmental details of Ruth's first year of life

114

were difficult to elicit from her mother, who had been anxiously preoccupied with the future fate of Ruth's congenital defect. Following a normal pregnancy and delivery, Ruth had been bottle-fed until age six months, when she began to spit out solids. Her mother, feeling this signaled a need for self-sufficiency in the entire feeding area, responded by allowing Ruth to feed herself and by abruptly withdrawing all bottle feeding. No particular sequelae were noted by the mother, although we observed a large variety of oral behaviors including mouthing and licking of objects and tongue protrusion and pulling when Ruth entered our nursery during her 12th month. The less-than-optimal recognition of Ruth's cues, as evidenced in the abrupt, probably traumatic weaning, proved to be characteristic of this mother's relationship with her child, and lent a particular quality to the developing object ties.

The pillow applied for correction of the congenital deformity was worn at all times, except during bathing and diapering; it placed a mild restriction upon leg motion, but had only slightly delayed motor development. Ruth stood with support at seven months, crawled at eight months, and walked with support at 14 months and without support at 16 months. Ruth had made a remarkable accommodation to the corrective device as she crawled about most efficiently.

Yet, in spite of a fairly smooth development in the motoric, perceptual, and cognitive areas, her developing object relations were of a peculiar nature. From her sixth month on, Ruth had suffered intense "stranger anxiety," the most striking elements of which were her visual hypervigilance and clinging to her mother's body. At about the same time she had developed a fear of the noise of the vacuum cleaner, of lying down in the tub to have her hair washed, and of her periodic physical examination for her congenital deformity. All except the fear of strangers and the fear of her pediatrician had disappeared by the time she entered our nursery at age 12 months. Her stranger anxiety was still so intense that it took several days before her staff observer could approach without eliciting serious distress even as Ruth sat on her mother's lap, a reaction which may have represented in part a revival of memories of the many upsetting pediatric examinations to which this infant had been subjected. We also learned from her mother that Ruth's way of mastering her separation anxiety was to fall asleep immediately when left with a neighbor for baby-sitting. We have consistently observed that many infants, when confronted by the strange people in the nursery, cling closely to the mother. Although they are not actually being threatened with separation, we believe we are witnessing an upsurge of separation, or object-loss anxiety. Ruth's reaction was, however, far more intense than that of any of the other infants.

We think that the persistent separation and stranger anxiety derived from several sources: first, Ruth perceived that the perineal pillow had been removed during each diapering and bathing. For an infant between three and 12 months of age, the removal of the pressure against the perineum probably produced sensations of intermittent loss of a quasi body part.[1] Second, the par-

------

[1] We are indebted to Phyllis Greenacre for suggesting that the softness of the pillow may have a limited breastlike quality, thereby intensifying the mouth-genital connection, a connection Greenacre has found more often in girls than in boys.

tial motor restriction produced by the pillow added to Ruth's difficulties in developing a concept of her body and limited her opportunities for aggressive motor discharge; and third, the mother's anxious concern about the deformity, along with her less-than-adequate mothering, resulted in some disturbance in Ruth's developing object relationships. In short, Ruth was experiencing more than the ordinary difficulty in establishing a relatively stable mental representation of the maternal object and of the self, the symptomatic expression of which was her intense separation and stranger anxiety which continued well beyond the average period.

From about 14 months of age Ruth began to practice many varieties of "object-disappearance" games, including the usual peek-a-boo, mirror peek-a-boo, repetitive toilet flushing, and repetitive use of the mailbox toy (in which forms are dropped through cut-out slats and then retrieved).

In her relationships with people, modest frustration evoked mild temper tantrums as well as focused hostility directed at other persons or at herself. She would, for example, scratch, bite, and tease her mother and her favorite staff member, or bite her own fingers. Focused affectionate behavior also appeared as Ruth kissed and hugged people, dolls, and other inanimate objects. In relation to certain aspects of ego functioning, we witnessed a spurt in her use of symbolic speech. Ruth acquired names for her parents and dolls which she soon used even in the absence of these objects. Semisymbolic play — placing dolls in bed, on the play toilet, etc. — began to appear when Ruth was 16 months old, at least two months later than many of her peers.

From the group of behaviors just described, we infer that more distinct and stable self as well as object representations were becoming established. As self and object differentiation proceeded, object-directed aggressive and affectionate behavior emerged, as well as a certain amount of self-directed aggression in the form of self-biting.

The increasing individuation was, however, accompanied by manifest anxiety, as indicated by an intensification of oral behavior. This included eating, as well as her earlier forms of thumb and object-sucking, and tongue-licking, pulling, and protrusion. Furthermore, Ruth's engagement in any new activity was contingent on a specific condition — the maintenance of direct visual contact with her mother at all times, which her peers of 16 months no longer needed. Yet, in spite of these evidences of more than usual anxiety, her chronically "anxious" searching look, with eyes slightly narrowed and gaze soon averted, now gradually gave way to a more open, bright expression, often with a trace of playful teasing. We infer from this that some greater stability of the mental self and object representations had been achieved.

At the appropriate age of 14 months Ruth could name her own facial features and appendages as well as those of her parents. She had been exposed to her mother's naked body from the beginning, but it was not until her 14th month, at the same time as focused hostile aggression and affection emerged, that she began to stare intently at her mother's breasts and pubic hair, as yet without attempting to touch them. It should be mentioned that her father, unlike her mother, had avoided undressing in Ruth's presence from her sixth month onward.

At about 14½ months, the umbilicus became the focus of Ruth's attention as part of a highly exciting reciprocal umbilicus-touching game with her mother. Soon afterward interest in anal functioning became evident as Ruth insisted upon being in the bathroom during her mother's toileting procedures, a common occurrence in all the families we have studied. She pointed to and developed a distinctive name for the stool in the toilet, and flushed the toilet repetitively both at home and in the nursery. All this took place in the absence of any effort at toilet training by the mother. At 16 months, when she had just begun independent walking, Ruth gestured that she wanted to see her stool in the soiled diaper which had just been removed from her. She then proceeded to sit on the toidy seat in the nursery while clothed. Shortly thereafter she acquired a distinctive word for urination, a step following the usual developmental progression from anal to urinary zone.

These behaviors indicated to us that there was increasingly stable mental representation of her own body. New themes appeared in her play activities. She stacked blocks to build high towers, piled toys into carriages and other receptacles, repetitively emptied drawers and shelves of their contents and then refilled them, performing all this in an orderly and deliberate manner, in contrast to her previous "throwing" style. She insisted that her toys remain just where she had put them, and now was able to take toys away from her peers and defend her own possessions.

The new organizational level of her play was, we inferred, evidence that the anal and urinary areas and functions were achieving more solid mental representation. Anal traits of possessiveness as well as some degree of elementary organization, demonstrated in Ruth's orderly arrangement of concrete objects and her interest in their spatial relationships, seemed to reflect the new level of personality organization.

The enormous surge in almost all areas of development which had begun at 14 months reached a climax during Ruth's 17th month, just one month after she had finally attained upright, unaided locomotion. She could now maintain distance from her mother as she engaged in social interchange; and her oral activities subsided remarkably. Furthermore, she held her own cup alone for the first time. Her sleep, which had been disturbed for several months, became peaceful, and she developed an attachment to a transitional object in the form of a "fuzzy dog" which was her constant nighttime companion. For the first time since the initial development of stranger anxiety during her sixth month, Ruth now greeted strangers without a trace of her former apprehension. This remarkable qualitative change in the nature of her object relations indicated to us that there was increasing reliability of the object representation, as a result of which her separation anxiety almost completely disappeared.

In the midst of the new-found pleasure and freedom of her early 17th month, evidence of Ruth's first focused genital interest was observed in the nursery and simultaneously reported by her mother. Her occasional fleeting gesture toward the genital area during diapering in the preceding month or so was now, at 17½ months, replaced by intentional genital handling during every diapering as she inserted two fingers between her labia. She crouched down and peered up between her widespread legs; undressed dolls, calling some of them "boy" for the first time; examined their perineal areas; and smilingly used the one family word which had been offered her for both genital and anal areas (again a common practice in the families we have studied). She tried to lift and peer beneath her mother's skirt and that of her favorite staff member. Her interest in the reciprocal umbilicus game dwindled, but the diapering of other nursery children, which Ruth had previously ignored, now became of great interest to her. She hovered about the toilet, pushed the potty seat about the nursery, and shadowed her mother whenever she entered the bathroom. From this behavior, we inferred that mental representation of the genital area and of the anatomical genital difference was being established, as we had had earlier evidence that she had been aware of urinary and anal functions and sensations.

Some three weeks after the onset of her genital curiosity, that is, at 18¼ months of age, subtle but pervasive changes in mood, in the nature of her object relationships, and in other aspects of ego functioning began to appear. On one occasion Ruth was watching with her usual interest the diapering of a boy in the nursery. Fully clothed, she then sat down on a toidy seat, holding a long xylophone stick perpendicularly against her perineal area, and displaying an odd look of uneasiness on her face. The toilet flush handle became of increasing interest to her as she fondled and licked it whenever she was near it. We could follow the pathway of displacement from the visual percept of the offending male genital itself to a variety of sites away from the body (by utilizing the type of analysis described in Chapter 5), as Ruth insistently and repetitively fingered knobs, car handles, and a variety of other protruding objects, which she now named "flush," a word previously reserved exclusively for the toilet handle.

Under the impact of her increasing anxiety about the observed sexual difference, distortion in verbal symbolization had occurred. The single attribute of phallic shape now united otherwise dissimilar objects under the common symbol, the word "flush." She was visibly disturbed by all broken toys, refusing to use broken crayons which had previously been entirely acceptable. We felt this behavior indicated that these toys had become invested with the significance of the two body zones with which she was now most concerned, the genital and anal, and a defect in the concrete external inanimate object that was thus invested could no longer be tolerated. It appeared that these two areas of ego functioning, play and speech, had suffered distortion through the increasing use of denial as she tried to cope with mounting anxiety. In the same manner, the toilet handle, which through displacement had come to represent the offending male genital, now evoked so much anxiety that its symbolic word designation was no longer maintained in a discrete form. Instead, the word "flush" was generalized to other phalliclike objects. This particular word symbol thus lost some of the specificity it had previously attained.

We have witnessed many instances of such invasions of ego functioning in connection with instinctual development and ongoing body schematization. Although these states are usually temporary, there is of course the possibility of a subtle and permanent influence on precisely those areas of ego functioning which are in the process of rapid development during the latter half of the second year of life: namely, developing symbolization both in the verbal and in the nonverbal areas. Visual symbolization in particular undergoes developmental elaboration at this age. One would therefore expect that stressful events occurring during this critical developmental period would leave permanent traces in the visual-perceptive area of functioning. Moreover, in this particular infant, the development of visual perception was probably even more complex than is usual, in view of the visual fixation which had been so impressive in her earlier stranger anxiety.

Ruth now engaged in new visual activities. She ran to look at any baby being diapered in the nursery, immediately thereafter glanced down at her own perineal area, and spoke her word for urination, indicating that the visual inspection involved a direct comparison. She became an intent window-gazer in the nursery, and was overheard murmuring "Daddy" on several occasions as she stared out at an empty street, seemingly occupied with fantasy. Her obvious concern with the genital differences exerted pressure on her parents, who now allowed her to witness her father's urination on several occasions. She seemed fascinated by the sight.

Her intense visual sexual curiosity seemed to combine with the sensations of genital arousal that she experienced as she witnessed diaperings and urinations. From this constellation an interesting group of phenomena emerged. Whenever she found someone looking at her, she blushed deeply and tried to hide her face. Simultaneously, she developed a new interest in all forms of fire such as her father's matches, her grandfather's barbecue, and fire engines. She repeated the words "hot" and "fire" in all these situations, and looked at the "hot" events with obvious fascination and clear signs of erotic excitement.

First, as to her "fiery" interest; Ruth had experienced genital sensations of localized arousal and warmth as she masturbated, sensations now retrospectively connected with her earlier oral perceptions of warmth. (Ruth's first word had been "hot," a warning used by her mother against burning her mouth with hot food.) In addition to the internal associative link, there was an external one in that the local genital warmth found an equivalent perceptual quality in the fires she observed and whose warmth she felt; and these fires in turn became linked with fire engines. All fiery events were thus equated with genital arousal, leading to the emergence of a new symbol: fire stood for sexual arousal. The connections between looking, sexual arousal, interest in fires, and the word "hot" had become established.

The phenomena of blushing and hiding her face on being looked at appear to relate to the matter of the developing sense of identity. Greenacre (1958) has emphasized the crucial role of the face and genitals, in contrast to other body areas, in establishing an image of one's own body self. Ruth's facial inspection had earlier been an important aspect of what we inferred to be her primitive attempts at self-object differentiation. As she now tackled this same task on a more complex level she avidly inspected genitals and objects to which genital displacement had taken place. It must be emphasized, however, that her earlier experiences had contributed a less than optimally firm body image.

The corrective device worn against the perineal area during the first year had surely aroused genital sensations, resulting in greater-than-average instability of genital schematization. Now, at one-and-a-half years, her new and acute awareness of genital arousal and the confusing comparisons of her own genitals with those of others constituted a new threat to the already distorted genital schematization. We speculate, therefore, that displacement occurred from the genital area to the face, which had been the site of the earlier efforts at identity establishment. Having become aroused as she visually inspected her father's genitals, she now became aroused when she was visually inspecting herself. Genital blushing and facial blushing were for the time being simultaneous phenomena, although we assumed that the genital aspect would soon become inhibited and eventually repressed. (The ready displacement from genital to face [Ferenczi, 1913] as well as the extensive employment of introjective-projective mechanisms are characteristic of psychic functioning during this developmental period.)

Toward the end of her 18th month, Ruth's comparisons and inspections of the genital area began to decrease; simultaneously a slow deterioration of her mood set in. The cheerfulness of her 17th month was replaced by irritability and decreasing frustration tolerance, but this time the aggression was not directed against the mother, as it had been at 15 months. Instead, she teased and provoked other adults and again began to bite her own fingers in a renewed emergence of self-directed aggression. The earlier fear of strangers and the clinging to her mother returned in ever-increasing intensity.

The mechanism of gradual displacement was evident as Ruth's attention turned upward from the offending genital zone to her former interest in her umbilicus. She repeatedly pushed her finger into it, lifted the clothing of our nursery dolls, and pointed at and named a nonexistent umbilicus, using the word "button," which was not the name her parents had used to designate this area. Many inanimate protuberances also became "buttons" in the same type of symbolic distortion we had observed during the period when she had first scrutinized the anatomical genital differences. As part of this effort to deny the genital difference by affirming the ubiquitous umbilicus in its place, Ruth tried to pin a safety pin on the abdomen of her favorite teddy bear.

In the midst of Ruth's mounting distress, her mother discovered that she was in the earliest months of a new pregnancy. Although we assume that this new event influenced Ruth's future development profoundly, her original distress had begun well in advance of any possible awareness of the pregnancy.

During one of her usual nursery sessions, Ruth bit ferociously on her own fingers and then chewed on the ear of a toy bear after she had witnessed the diapering of an infant girl. She had chewed and macerated a similar toy bear's ear at home a few days previously. On yet another morning, she was being supported in the arms of her staff observer for a better view of an infant boy's diapering which she had rushed to observe. Suddenly she averted her gaze, pulled off first one of the observer's earrings and then the other and gestured her wish to be put down on the floor. Running into the adjacent bathroom, she tore off toilet paper, dropped it into the toilet, and then tried to flush it away as she simultaneously licked at the flush handle.

We understood this behavior as indicating a wish to dispose of protrusions. Avoidance and displacement mechanisms were increasingly in evidence as her gaze avoided the perineal areas of dolls whose abdomens she diligently examined for the "button." She was more and more distressed by broken or imperfect toys, pointing at their defects, and actually using the word "broken." And a new fear of falling objects, particularly if they caused spattering or splashing, emphasized her awareness of the urinary aspect of the male genital. Temper tantrums returned; her sleep was once again disturbed, and the "toy dog" transitional object, which had been her obligatory nighttime companion, now became a daytime necessity as well. In addition, a new obligatory object made its appearance in the form of a doll which Ruth called "boy." She insisted that this doll, which resembled her other girl dolls in every way, be seated next to her at all meals and that "he" receive a mouthful of food each time she fed herself.

In attempting to understand the meaning of these

new developments, we assumed that Ruth had arrived at only marginal stability in the maternal object representation, compromised during her early months by the sudden weaning, the less than optimal mother-child relationship, and the limitation of aggressive motor discharge in consequence of the corrective device she wore. Now her awareness of the genital difference and the additional burden of anger and disappointment at her lack of a penis resulted in a split in the maternal image, with projection of the bad object. Recrudescence of the fear of strangers indicated a renewed fear of object loss, which followed the weakening of the maternal object representation through splitting. Simultaneously, a split in the self representation seemed to have occurred, with the obligatory toy dog and the doll "boy" representing split-off portions of Ruth's self-image.

As this critical period continued, inhibition of genital curiosity was soon reflected in a narrowing of her recently enlarged area of general curiosity. Ruth turned from her recent rich doll play to play with toys that involved the solution of tasks related to spatial relationships as well as anal functioning. The use of such toys had been the most prominent aspect of her early play. Now she again began to stack blocks, pile toys on top of one another within all kinds of receptacles, and use the "shape box" repetitively. This restriction of general curiosity paralleled the growing inhibition of Ruth's interest in toileting. She lost interest in the toilet and conspicuously avoided all references to the genital, anal, and urinary functions and areas. In sharp contrast, her interest in the toilet flush handle itself intensified, and she now used the word "flush" to designate the entire toilet, the opening and closing of doors, the electric light switch, and the brake of her carriage. All of these objects and situations shared the element of control rather than that of phallic shape, which had characterized her earlier symbolic distortion.

Her favorite inanimate companions were no longer the toy dog, but a number of dolls which she carried along without using them in play, one of which she named "baby." It seemed that Ruth had begun to use the concrete doll to take the place of the longed-for phallus. Her use of the name "baby" for this doll-phallus signals the establishment of a very early phallus-baby equation.

Ruth's worsening sleep disturbance reached its peak during her father's unusual absence from home over a period of several nights. She wept bitterly as she called for her mother, repeating her distinctive words for urination and defecation. She was inconsolable throughout the night. The following morning she deposited a stool in her newly acquired toidy seat for the first time, after which she stood up, gazed at the stool in amazement, and promptly urinated on the floor.

This acute reaction to the father's absence should be viewed against the background of the severe early stranger and separation anxiety which had waned and now had returned. With the temporary loss of the father, the fear of maternal loss was rekindled, and Ruth's defecation in the toidy seemed to represent a final surrender to her mother's wishes as she parted with the stool-phallus.

As if in vague recognition of the meaning of Ruth's gift of her stool, her frantic parents decided to purchase on that day a carriage and baby doll which she had been requesting for some time. With the carriage at her bedside and the doll in her arms, Ruth had her first quiet night in several weeks. Her last audible word as she fell asleep was "flush!" It was Ruth's attachment to the doll and carriage that first drew our attention to the fetishistic significance of such attachments (see Chapter 10).

Ruth's dramatic first surrender of her stool ushered in a period of relative "submission" in other areas of behavior, although she refused to use the toidy seat itself for many weeks therafter. Subdued and even sad at times, she was no longer interested in the toidy seat, the toilet and its flush, or in her father's showering to which she had rushed excitedly at every opportunity. All genital, anal, and urinary exploration and curiosity had ceased in relation to her own body, the diapering of other children, and her parents.

The toys she now played with were small toy horses which she placed at either side of her as she sat rocking in a small chair. She clung to the baby doll and its carriage. Broken toys and crayons continued to distress her, and she refused to use them.

At 22 months Ruth was a quiet child whose constant eating companions were the two dolls at her sides, Ruth insisting that they be fed while she fed herself. Her former anxious look of the narrowed eyes and tense face in the presence of strangers returned, and her curiosity became definitely limited in scope. The recognition of a definitive change in mood was her mother's first clear statement that Ruth would probably always be a "quiet" one who would be "afraid of strangers."

We are unable to assess the importance of the mother's new pregnancy and of the father's absence from home at such a crucial period of development in this infant's life, although we were able to verify that the castration reaction itself had begun well before the mother's conscious knowledge of her pregnancy.

Ruth's congenital defect, the need for repeated medical examinations, and the wearing of a corrective device undoubtedly interfered with the development of a stable mental representation of her mother and of her body self. Yet, with the development of free locomotion, there was a spurt in individuation and in symbolic development between Ruth's 14th and 17th months, as evident in the disappearance of stranger anxiety, the emergence of symbolic play, and in her enlarging verbal capacity. This ongoing individuation process brought her in due time to the awareness of anal, urinary, and genital anatomy and function, along with their appropriate sensations.

In this already vulnerable girl, the discovery of the sexual anatomical difference and sexual sensations brought with them overwhelming disappointment and anger at the mother, with loss of self-esteem and the marked inhibited and depressive reaction that continued to characterize her. The incomplete and unstable fusion of the good and bad maternal images was split, and the bad image was projected onto other figures. A basic mistrust prevailed, and we expected her to continue to have difficulties in separating from her mother. Another consequence of the distorted development of body schematization and object relations was a concurrent split in the mental representation of her own body (the doll "boy" and eating companion) and a weakening of several aspects of ego functioning (such as general curiosity, play, and symbolization).

Ruth's very early object relations, her sense of individual identity, and certain aspects of other ego functioning appear to have been indelibly affected by body experiences in her first year. We observed the impact of the discovery of the sexual anatomical difference during her second year and have attempted to delineate the consequences for defensive organization, object relations, mood, and style of play behavior.

Nine months after Ruth left the nursery, we had a report on her. A sister was born when Ruth was 26½ months old. Ruth seemed fond of the new baby and initially showed no hostility toward her. Just after the baby returned home, Ruth showed a spurt in doll play, but soon she abandoned it almost completely. Blocks became her favorite toy and the Empire State Building her favorite block-building project.

Toilet training had been accomplished before the baby sister was born. Although speech was advanced, the use of the personal pronoun "I" had not yet been achieved. Ruth continued to show marked anxiety in relation to even minor injuries. On one occasion she insisted on wearing long trousers to cover her scraped knee, long after the bandage had been removed. Following an injury to her lip she refused to eat for three days and made persistent attempts to hide her face from the view of others. And her tolerance of separation continued to be well below the expected level.

In summary, Ruth's earlier difficulties in the areas of self-esteem, object relations, and other aspects of ego functioning, such as nonverbal and verbal symbolization, were still in evidence as she entered the oedipal period; and the castration anxiety of her second year of life had not disappeared.

CHAPTER 7

THE NARCISSISTIC MOTHER

We have so far described severe castration reactions and some of the traumatic circumstances we believe responsible for these reactions. We now describe a more moderate reaction. To the best of our knowledge, Suzy did not suffer from any acute trauma in her first year and was not among our preselected infants. She did, however, suffer from the protracted trauma of having a not-good-enough mother. This case illustrates the circular nature of the mother-child interaction. An extremely narcissistic woman, the mother was able to provide adequately enough for Suzy's needs as long as the infant's development proceeded smoothly. But when Suzy began to show anxiety and disturbance consequent to observing the anatomical difference, the mother reacted with anger and her capacity for empathy broke down. Her disapproval of Suzy in turn exacerbated Suzy's castration reaction.

134

Suzy

When she entered the program, Suzy was a dainty, small-boned infant of 13 months. She had already worked as a photographer's model for many months and was capable not only of making the rounds of the modeling agencies with her mother in a quiet, poised manner but also of sitting through one- or two-hour sessions of photographing, patiently doing as she was told. Her birth was normal; her early development was reported as "good." She had been walking for three months when she first came to the nursery and was surefooted and agile.

Suzy was an only child. Her mother, an attractive young woman who worked intermittently as an actress, had gained 45 pounds during her pregnancy. In the early months she had been so eager to show that she was pregnant, she had worn maternity clothes long before they were necessary. She dressed herself and Suzy with style and flare. She experienced her daughter as an extension of herself, was proud of her little girl's appearance, and reacted grievously to each bruise, cut, or scar her daughter suffered. Suzy's father, energetic and ambitious, was evidently a loving and devoted husband and father.

At 13 and 14 months Suzy showed very little interest in her genitals. Occasionally, when exposed during the changing of her diapers, she would touch her genitals, but this activity seemed of no more importance to her than her curiosity about the rest of her body. At 15 months she suddenly began to show definite and pervasive curiosity about the genitals of other children. As soon as any infant was taken to the changing table at the nursery, Suzy would come over and watch intently as the diaper was being changed. No matter what she was doing, she never missed an opportunity to witness the whole procedure. Regardless of how involved she was in any activity, there always seemed to be some measure of attention focused on the changing table. In all other ways, in her interests and play, she seemed no different from any of the other infants.

The first time Suzy's interest in the changing table was observed, a little boy of about her own age was being changed after a bowel movement. He touched his penis and pulled at it during the process. Suzy, with her eyes riveted on the boy's genitals, pointed to his penis and then touched herself, through her diaper, in the genital area. She then began to wipe the area with a paper towel. Her mother took it away from her, but Suzy quickly got another. On subsequent occasions when she watched a little boy being changed, she either tried to touch his penis or pointed to it and then either touched her genital area if fully clothed or her genital directly if she were being changed and was exposed. Her mother always tried to stop her by taking away the towel with which she wiped herself, by removing her hands from her genitals when she began to masturbate, or by placing her on the toilet when she clutched her genital area, apparently assuming that Suzy had to urinate.

During this same period, when a little girl was being changed, Suzy would watch intently but without pointing or making any effort to touch the genitals of the little girl. Then she would clutch her buttocks, which we interpreted as an incipient denial of the anatomical difference between the sexes by way of displacement to the rear. This distinction in Suzy's responses persisted over several months.

When Suzy was 17 months old, she began to lift her skirt and giggle excitedly. During this same period she often tried to lift the skirts of the women in the nursery, never the little girls, and tried to peer under their dresses. She did the same at home to her mother who became quite upset by this behavior. It was only then that we learned that Suzy had been showering regularly with both her father and mother since the age of 12 or 13 months. We were unable to learn whether she had ever made any effort to touch her father's penis or to explore her mother's pubic area. However, her intense curiosity about the genital anatomy of adult women probably reflected perplexity from having seen pubic hair. The difference between her genital and her mother's may have raised the question of whether her mother had a penis hidden somewhere. Her mother, apparently with some appreciation of the relationship between Suzy's recent sexual curiosity and the experience of exposure, discontinued the joint showers.

As we said earlier, so long as her little daughter was passive, compliant, and showed off well, the mother was able to read her cues and provide for her needs. When Suzy developed a will of her own, however, and seemed to react to the narcissistic insult from having observed the anatomical difference between the sexes, discord developed between mother and daughter. When Suzy began to shower with her parents, she also started to hold food in her mouth while being fed. Her cheeks puffed, she retained the food in spite of her mother's mounting irritation. We speculate that this behavior was related to a fantasy of acquiring a penis by eating one.

The timing of the appearance of Suzy's sexual curiosity and her sexual behavior are common to all of the infants we have studied, no matter what their experiences have been. It is possible, however, that the intensity of Suzy's sexual curiosity was stimulated by her early and repeated exposure to her nude parents. As we have already stated, the level of parental body exposure to their babies came as something of a surprise to us. Some degree of regular parental exposure seems to be ubiquitous from the latter half of the first year on, regardless of social, economic, or cultural differences. Virtually all our mothers, having no regular domestic help with whom to leave their babies, use the toilet with the children in the bathroom. Although the fathers' exposure is much more variable and by no means as regular, we have accumulated many instances in which fathers exposed themselves while urinating before their 14- to 16-month-old daughters, just at the time the little girls are actively turning to the fathers and also at a time when some incipient genital arousal ordinarily begins.

Before proceeding with the further vicissitudes of Suzy's sexual attitudes and behavior, we should (because of the close connection between the two aspects of development) review the history of her toilet training. From the age of eight months, her mother had placed her on the toilet after breakfast and lunch, without much success. The family word for urination was "tee-

tee" and for bowel movements, "blinkie." (This unusual word was derived from the parents' observation that Suzy blinked her eyes when she had a bowel movement.) By the age of 17 months, she was already using these words either in an anticipatory fashion or to indicate that she had already wet or soiled herself. When she used the toilet, her parents would applaud, make a big fuss, and wave bye-bye to the bowel movement. Over a period of a month she attained reasonably reliable sphincter control, particularly over her bowel movements.

At 18 to 19 months of age, after some six weeks of established toilet control, Suzy developed confusion in language concerning toilet activities. She began to say "blinkies" when her diaper was wet or when she held her genital area, usually a signal that she had to urinate. At other times she would lift her skirt in front in an exhibitionistic manner and say "hiny," a word which she had consistently used earlier to refer to her buttocks.

Suzy's behavior should be viewed against the background of our observations of how children learn to name the parts of the body. In our sample, all the boys by the age of 18 to 19 months had been told the words for the penis and the buttocks, for urination and bowel movements. Up through the second year, none of the boys had been given a term for the scrotum or testes, although by this time most of them showed some interest in these body parts (cf., Bell, 1961). The girls, although they were given separate and distinct names for toilet functions and for the buttocks, were not given any discrete word for their genitals. Only after their little girls show intense sexual curiosity do a few mothers give them a word for their genitals. We believe that to omit naming such an important part of the body reflects a cultural manifestation of the castration complex. It suggests how early and how fundamentally cultural attitudes toward little boys and girls diverge (cf., Abraham, 1911; see also Lerner, 1976).

To return to Suzy's sexual curiosity and behavior, let us consider the developing confusion over body parts and functions that arose when she was 18 to 19 months old. In addition to her interest in the activities at the diapering table and her peering under women's skirts, she showed much more intense sexual activity and exploration. Until the age of 19 months she engaged in genital masturbation when in the bath or on the changing table. Whenever she saw her mother's breasts, she touched them and was often seen touching or pulling her own nipples.

In the nursery, Suzy often undressed the dolls, scrutinized the area between their legs, and then said "hiny." This doll play became increasingly elaborate: she pretended to shower the doll, placed her on the toilet to have a bowel movement, wiped her, and then washed her hands. Her play reflected the underlying concerns about her own body that Suzy was struggling with at this time.

At 19 months, there was an abrupt cessation of most of this sexual activity. She no longer went to the changing table to watch the other children while they were exposed. She no longer made any effort to peer under women's skirts. All of her genital masturbatory activity stopped. The only behavioral remnant, which was probably a derivative of the earlier sexual interest, was a persistent tendency to touch her mother's buttocks and breasts as well as her own.

The confusion that had started some two months earlier about naming body parts and functions now, at 19 months, became consistent. The word for urination dropped out of her vocabulary entirely. When she used the toilet to urinate, she wiped her buttocks. Earlier, when she wished to refer to her genitals, she had used the functional name "tee-tee"; now she always referred to it as her "hiny." During this time she developed a mild anxiety when the toilet flushed. This anxiety varied in intensity over the ensuing months. She also developed transitory and shifting fears of birds, dogs, horses, and other animals. From time to time she was seen scrutinizing her finger or leg with some apprehension, dolefully saying "boo-boo" — her word for a cut or sore — when, as a rule, no sign of injury was apparent.

When Suzy was almost 20 months old, a little boy her own age spent the day with his mother at her house. She followed him into the bathroom when he went to urinate, reached out to touch his penis, and said, "Pee-pee," a word neither she nor her mother had ever used to refer to either the penis or urination. For several days after this experience all the earlier sexual behavior — going to the changing table, touching her own genitals and masturbating, lifting skirts, etc. — flared up again but in a short while disappeared. On three other occasions over the next several months when a boy visited and she had the opportunity to witness him urinating, this behavior reappeared briefly.

It is an unfortunate limitation of the observational method that children so young have limited verbal capacity. Accordingly, the meaning of such an intriguing detail of behavior as Suzy's consistent tendency, whenever she saw a little boy's penis exposed, to either point or reach out to touch it, must remain open to question. Perhaps it reflects some shocklike response to the perception of the anatomical difference between the sexes (cf., Greenacre, 1956) with some effort to establish through touch that the penis is real; or it may already betray a partially inhibited aggressive impulse to take the penis.

It is possible, we feel, that both interpretations may be true. Suzy's persistent need to repeat the observation of the penis over and over again in a relatively unvarying manner suggests that she reacted to the sight of the penis in a traumatic fashion. The repetitiveness seems to point to a need to establish the reality of the percept. The tendency to touch the penis suggests an effort to reinforce the visual perception by using a more primitive perceptual modality. That this same behavior may also serve the fantasy of aggressively grasping and acquiring the penis seems equally probable and entirely in keeping with the principle of multiple determination of behavior. In a similar fashion, clutching the buttocks when she saw a little girl's genitals, referring to her genitals as a "hiny," dropping the word for urination, and subsequently using the word for a bowel movement to signal urinary urgency, all seem to point to a profound denial of the genital difference, that is, a shift away from the genital area to the anal area, which is, of course, the same in both sexes. At the same time, this behavior seems to signify an incipient restitutive fantasy along the lines of the well-known stool-penis equation (Abraham, 1920, p. 343). In any event, it seems likely that Suzy's wide array of behavioral phenomena reflects a moderately severe castration reaction. Our interpretation of Suzy's development is supported by the emergence of the fear of the flush of the toilet, fear of animals, and her scrutinizing her body for cuts and wounds. These transitory and shifting fears may herald the later fixed phobic reactions of the phallic-oedipal phase and are a consequence of the displacements and projections of castration concerns onto other parts of the body and the external world. The general body-castration hypochondria as reflected in the anxious preoccupation with real or imagined cuts and bruises reflects this displacement of castration concerns away from the genital area onto other body parts. The projected castration anxiety is reflected in the fear of the toilet flush; the anxiety about the disappearance and loss of the stool product is a consequence of the common defensive displacement of castration concerns onto the anal zone and the stool product. The transitory and shifting nature of these fears during the early genital phase as contrasted with the fixed phobic reactions of the later phallic-oedipal phase reflects the relative lack of cohesiveness of ego structures at this time as compared with their greater stability and integrity in the phallic-oedipal phase.

By the time Suzy was 20 months of age, there was a complete deterioration of her toilet control, which persisted over the next few months. Her mother's irritation over this lapse in control was considerable. It seems to us that the deterioration of toilet control was a direct outcome of castration anxiety. Confirmation of the castration concern was seen in Suzy's statement to her mother, "Michael has a pee-pee. I have no pee-pee. Why?"

This case illustrates how bowel and bladder control in the second year may break down as a consequence of castration anxiety. One of the unexpected findings of our research has been that the whole process of toilet training is subject to the influence of the "minor" castration insults such as an infant of this age may quite readily come by in the ordinary course of events. For example, a little boy sees his mother exposed and is constipated for several days; a little girl whose bladder control has been reasonably reliable for some time sees a boy urinate and begins to wet for about a week. We have been accustomed to think about the toilet-training situation as something that the child does for the parents. Thus the training experience is interpreted rigidly in terms of the struggle for independence that is characteristic of this phase of development. We wish to add that the vicissitudes of the child's sexual interests, curiosity, and activity, also typical of this period, appear to have an influence upon the whole toilet-training process and may perhaps be at the center of some of the psychopathology that begins at this time.

The deterioration of Suzy's control of her bowels and bladder was followed by a profound general behavioral regression and negativism. When she came to the nursery, she refused to get out of her stroller. Sitting there for a considerable time looking sullen and distressed, she would not permit her mother or the nursery teacher to remove her jacket. She screamed if any of the children tried to touch her. When she was finally coaxed out of her stroller, she stayed close to her mother. If her mother was momentarily out of sight, Suzy panicked. Sullenly mistrustful of other adults and children, she could not be comforted unless her mother picked her up. A strong contrast, indeed, to the confident, competent, cheerful little girl of only a few months before who came into the nursery eager and smiling and sought out children or adults quite independently of her mother. And the mother — perplexed, frustrated, angry — reacted as if her self-esteem had been wounded. She responded sharply and harshly to Suzy's clinging, which hardly augured well for Suzy's future development in the area of object relations.

Thus we see that the process of sexual arousal and the discovery of the anatomical difference between the sexes produced a castration reaction which affected this infant's psychic development. Her anger and disappointment with her mother are reflected in the almost paralyzing hostile dependence on her that developed. This accretion of aggression tends to threaten the cohesiveness of the ego, tends to threaten the integrity of the crucial self and object representation, and seems to call forth the early defense mechanisms of splitting the good and bad mother images and turning the aggression against the self (Mahler, 1971).

Concurrent with the undermining of Suzy's developing object relations is the indication of an interference with and weakening of several other aspects of the maturing ego functioning. Most dramatic was the pervasive inhibition of her curiosity in general and of her sexual curiosity in particular; parallel with this was a marked inhibition and regressive deterioration of play. Her earlier play with dolls rapidly became constricted and all but disappeared. An outstanding effect of Suzy's castration anxiety was a loss in self-esteem and the emergence of a depressive mood.

The developmental disturbances we have described are certainly consistent with the picture Mahler (1966; Mahler et al., 1975) draws of the rapprochement subphase, especially the rapprochement crisis. With regard to both timing and behavior, Suzy seemed to show just such a crisis. Mahler (Mahler et al., 1975) finds the rapprochement crisis more common and more dramatic in the little girl than in the little boy. We have found preoedipal castration reactions much more frequently in girls than in boys. We suggest that one of the significant dynamic factors that precipitate the rapprochement crisis in the latter half of the second year is the castration reaction following the early genital-zone arousal.

CHAPTER 8

THE DEPRESSED MOTHER

Severe postpartum depression or significant chronic depression in the mother presents the developing infant with a major challenge in its efforts to forge a basic attachment to the human object world. The mother of the baby we describe in this chapter was chronically depressed and suffered a sharp intensification of her depression with the birth of her baby. In addition, the infant had to deal with a series of actual separations regularly spaced throughout the second year, separations that were, we believe, intimately related to the mother's core depression.

These experiences resulted in a child who, by the time she was two years old, was unable to function outside the narrow orbit of her mother and was unable to develop the age-appropriate libidinal investment of her relationship to her father. She manifested a persistent depressive mood and, in spite of extraordinary endowment, was seriously constricted in her symbolic play.

Her libidinal and aggressive drive organization was markedly distorted as reflected in a profound ambivalence and a precocious erotization of aggression.

JODY

Jody was just under a year old when she and her mother started attending our research nursery. She was a chubby, blonde, blue-eyed, pretty little girl whose most remarkable feature was an intent visual alertness. While she showed some moderate reaction, as do all of our babies at first, to the strange physical surroundings and the many strange adults and children, none of us felt that her intent gaze was simply a reflection of a still active stranger anxiety.

Her attractive mother was a stiff, uneasy, anxious, and chronically depressed woman who at 26 had already been married for seven years before the birth of this first child. She said that she had been for so long used to care only for herself that she found the demandingness of a new baby much more difficult and disrupting than did most new mothers.

Jody's mother, an only child, had been born in Nazi-occupied Holland. Her Jewish family lived in hiding, constantly under the threat of being discovered. Indeed, when she was one and a half years old her father was apprehended, sent to a concentration camp, and subsequently killed. When she was three years old she was separated from her mother and rarely saw her until they were reunited at the end of the war.

Both Jody's parents had consciously wished for a boy child. After delivery, the mother experienced a profound depression, with severe fatigue and contentless bouts of crying, which raged acutely for the first four months of her baby's life. Because of this depression, Jody at age 10 weeks was abruptly weaned to a bottle in 48 hours and left in the care of her paternal grandparents while her parents took a vacation for two weeks.

When Jody was four months old, the acute aspects of her mother's depression lifted. Still chronically anxious and depressed, she nevertheless seemed to find the care of her infant somewhat easier and experienced increasing pleasure in her pretty baby. Whereas up to this time Jody had only rarely given any sign of recognizing her mother, now the mother could count on getting a smile from her. Jody also now manifested a distinct stranger reaction. By the unusually early age of six months she spontaneously initiated a peek-a-boo game, which continued to be a favorite of hers. By this same time she had already developed a remarkable gestural and facial imitation of her mother and also imitatively reproduced several words.

The primary consequence of the mother's depression was a marked delay in attachment to the maternal object as reflected in the delay in a social smiling response to the mother and an early stranger reaction. Whether the lifting of the mother's depression at this time facilitated or was a consequence of these crucial developments is one of those chicken-and-egg questions. In any case, the emergence of the stranger reaction indicated that differentiation was proceeding precociously.

By nine months Jody had a spontaneous and appropriately used vocabulary of about six words, her speech continued to be precocious, and she was also showing interest in her mirror image. Within a month she was, on being asked by her mother, pointing to her eyes, nose, mouth, hand, feet, fingers, and toes.

At 12 months she displayed intense fear of a teddy bear whose eyes rolled with a change of position and of a wind-up toy monkey, both inanimate objects having independent motion.

When Jody was four months old she regularly clutched her mother's long hair when the mother was bent over her in feeding or diapering, an act the mother felt was aggressive, even at this early stage. By nine months, however, it was clearly hostile; several babies with whom Jody came in contact were already frightened by her hair-pulling attacks.

By the time Jody started in the nursery she had already been confronted with major stresses in her development and had demonstrated precocious capacities to squeeze out of a rather arid environment whatever nutriment she could. While she experienced a major deprivation of maternal emotional availability in her early months, she did succeed in forging an attachment to the maternal object. This was undoubtedly accomplished under strain and with some fundamental instability in her basic attachment to the object world. The unusually early pronounced imitative behavior bespeaks a marked intensification of primary identification mechanisms in the service of bolstering the wavering attachment to the maternal object who was in reality not predictably available. The precocious, spontaneously initiated peek-a-boo play further confirms the early structuralization of the ego in its efforts at actively mastering her central object-loss concerns (Kleeman, 1967). The early mirror-image fascination and conscious awareness of body parts reflect a premature body-self differentiation which complements the differentiation of a representation of the primal object.

Jody's fear of inanimate objects having an independent movement, such as the wind-up monkey, which was observed when she was 12 to 13 months, although quite common in children of seven to nine months, usually disappears or diminishes in an infant of that age. We believe that the "monkey fear" points to the emergence of the primal discrimination of animate-inanimate. Jody seems to have sensed that the monkey was inanimate, and fear arose from her childish equation of independent motion with living forms; clearly this infant must have been very sensitized to this confusion in view of her mother's frequent withdrawn, depressive states.

Emde (1976) presents a somewhat different explanation for the emergence of fear of the strange. He believes that the emergence of fearfulness reflects a maturationally determined general organismic shift to a new level of organization in the emotional, social, and physiological sectors. The new level of emotional organization permits the infant to communicate fear and bespeaks a heightened preference for the mother; in expressing fearfulness, the infant clearly communicates: "I feel secure only with you, mother. Don't leave me unprotected in strange, threatening situations."

Emde's discussion, with its emphasis on the biological determination of the monkey fear, does not really quarrel with ours. The capacity for the expression of fear may be biologically determined, but we are addressing ourselves to the psychological resonance of the fear, which invests it with a meaning that reflects a line of developing object relatedness, and in response to specific experiences with a seriously withdrawn, depressed mother.

This leads to one final but very important detail in Jody's development in the first year, the early emergence of hostile aggression. The reflexive hair-pulling at four months is entirely normal and part of such biological givens as the sucking reflex and rooting behavior, which form the nucleus of attachment behavior. Early stroking or fingering of the mother's hair during feeding seems to be a forerunner of later transitional-object and transitional-phenomena behavior which emerges out of the positive libidinal attachment. The descriptions of the feeding situations at four months strongly suggest that the infant's hair-pulling was an effort to gain the mother's attention when she was emotionally withdrawn in her depression. What was perhaps unusual was the mother's perception of this as aggressive behavior, a response which we assume was a projection of the mother's own hostility toward the infant. However, the persistence and expansion of the hair-pulling in the latter half of the first year, its intentional quality, and the accompanying smile as Jody continued to pull her mother's hair and to crawl after other children in order to do the same, did signify its emergence as a distinct and intentionally directed aggressive act.

We share Winnicott's view (1969) that, as the infant differentiates, he (or she) places the object outside of his omnipotent control; that is, when the infant experiences the object as external to himself, he experiences a sense of loss (of the symbiotic object) which inevitably seems to evoke an increase of object-directed aggression. The following developmental material on Jody offers support of Winnicott's views.

When Jody started at the nursery two weeks before her first birthday, she could pull herself to an upright posture and manage to walk with support, but her exclusive mode of getting about was an active, rapid crawl. Her vocabulary in the nursery was unusually large, and even more extensive at home. We observed her fascination with her mirror image and the detailed discrimination of body parts both on herself and her dolls.

Jody started to sleep through the night regularly a short time after she was one month old. The going-to-sleep ritual was of more than passing interest. From the time she was first regularly fed a bottle at 10 weeks, and during the entire time the couple attended the nursery, the mother held Jody in her arms for feeding. Sitting on a straight-back chair, the mother rocked Jody in her arms until Jody was drowsy and then put her down in the crib. Jody was never given the bottle in the crib, which, however, always contained a pacifier which she sometimes sucked but most often just held. She occasionally stroked her own hair or fingered the bed sheets, but she never developed an attachment to a transitional object.

Shortly before Jody was 13 months her parents again left her at the grandparents' apartment for two weeks. Familiar with both her grandparents, she had a particularly warm relationship with her doting grandfather, and seemed to fare quite well there except when she was occasionally shown a picture of her mother, when she would burst out crying, and dolefully call, "Momma, momma." On her parents' return she smiled and, after a moment's hestitation, rushed into her mother's arms. But when her mother put on her coat preparatory to taking the infant home, Jody burst into tears and was inconsolable until she herself was dressed. Over the next few weeks she continued to show marked anxiety whenever her mother put on her coat and on several occasions jumped when she heard the door slam.

The first night Jody spent at home in her own crib, a major sleep disturbance erupted and persisted in varying degrees over the following eight months that we continued to follow her. During the four-week period of acute sleep disturbance, she awoke, frequently in a state of panic, as many as seven or eight times a night. She was allowed to stay up several hours past her usual bedtime until she was so fatigued that she could hardly resist going to sleep. Fussing extended to the preliminary nighttime routine, and for the first week or two she even resisted and often refused her naps. She began to insist that the door to her bedroom, which heretofore had always been closed, be left open.

Some three weeks later the mother, frantic with fatigue and worry, asked us what she could do to improve this situation. We suggested that she try putting Jody down in her crib to sleep with her bottle instead of holding her in her arms. That night she tried this altered routine, and the child slept through the night. However, the next night the mother resumed the usual routine of holding Jody in her arms, saying, "If she can go to sleep with the bottle, she can go to sleep without it." Although this did not turn out to be the case, the mother never again attempted the altered routine we suggested.

Almost immediately following her parents' return, Jody developed a cold, temperature elevation, and diarrhea which lasted for about a week. The alteration in her mood was highly dramatic and persisted in an acute form for a month after the separation. She seemed anxious and cranky; she shadowed her mother, literally clinging to her, and frequently asked to be picked up. After a few days, a rampant aggression seemed to explode. While hugging her mother at bedtime, she would suddenly bite her shoulder. With equal suddenness she would fiercely pinch, slap, and pull hair. For the first time, teasing behavior became prominent. Although her mother was the principal target, Jody also attacked her observers, the nursery teachers, other children, and her dolls, especially when she was in any way frustrated. Her relations to other children were curiously inconsistent. While she never made any effort to defend herself against attack or to retrieve or hold onto a toy that another child took away, she repeatedly and without provocation clutched a fistful of another child's hair and fiercely pulled it. Her fingers had to be forcefully pried open, and if the other child cried in pain Jody would stare intently, her face often showing empathic sorrow. She frequently swallowed the hair she succeeded in pulling out — her mother said that Jody had a very regular diet of this hair. Her food intake was sharply diminished so that her only regular source of nutrition was the milk she took in her bottles, and this heretofore neat and dainty little girl would now sit in her highchair and mess with the food on her plate instead of eating.

Jody did not begin to walk regularly until she was close to 16 months, although she showed reasonably steady balance when standing unsupported, and even managed a few steps. A number of observers had the distinct impression that her balance was good enough long before she began to walk, but that she "didn't want to." For a month before she herself walked, she was frequently observed to "walk" her dolls and was heard to say, "Doll, walk."

In the six-week period following the separation from her parents, her anal, urinary, and genital awareness and preoccupation increased sharply, along with a continued and expanding general body exploration. She had an unusual interest in eyes — her own, her parents', and dolls' — and not only used the word "eye" but also named the lashes. She continued to be fascinated with her mirror image, exploring her naked body in the mirror and, rather remarkably in one so young, identified her mirror image as "Jody."

Before the separation, Jody had shown some rudimentary awareness of bowel and bladder function, as well as some patterning of her activity by these functions. Beginning immediately after the separation and continuing over the next three weeks, she consistently tugged at her diaper after a bowel movement and verbally signaled that she had one by saying "Caca." Her interest in the bathroom and in her mother's toilet functions were manifest for the first time. Her mother's response to this new interest was to admonish her with the word "dirty." She continued to bring tiny bits of paper, lint, or soot from the floor to her mother and, now saying "dirty," would throw them into the wastebasket. She climbed into small spaces — the toy shelf, under cabinets and into corners — sometimes while having a bowel movement but often at other times as well. A favorite new activity was an endless stuffing of objects into containers and then emptying them. At this time Jody became constipated for a few days and, after she finally succeeded in having a bowel movement, said, "Caca, dada, bye-bye." After this she began to resist diaper changes vigorously for some time after she had had a bowel movement, verbalizing her resistance with a very decided "No." She also began to hide objects that belonged to her mother.

Just after her parents had returned from their vacation, Jody had discovered her genitals, and over the next several weeks touched them with gradually increasing frequency. Although she had previously had many opportunities to see her father's exposed penis, she now pointed to it for the first time and said "nipple," her word for her mother's breast, and she now named her own genitals "gina." She showed a sharply increased interest in her mother's and father's genitals and pubic hair and began to reach out and touch them. She increasingly began to look down and reach into her mother's blouse, saying "nipple," and on several occasions asking, "Gina?" after this exploration. She began to laugh now when her mother playfully blew on her perineum during diaper changes. In the nursery she seemed fascinated with a toy rubber elephant, frequently pulling its trunk, but she refused to call the elephant by name, an unusual feature in this highly verbal infant.

It was both fascinating and moving to observe the interactional details by which Jody's narcissistic, depressed mother communicated her own highly disturbed object relatedness to her relatively helpless infant. The characteristic going-to-sleep ritual had a most interesting texture. In this most intense and paradigmatic mother-child interaction, the feeding situation, Jody' mother offered her baby the maximum of tactile and kinesthetic closeness before that quintessential situation of object loss: going to sleep. But in the final transition to sleep, the baby was entirely alone without even that ordinary indication of the mother's presence, the bottle. This baby did spontaneously develop some rudimentary transitional behavior, such as holding the pacifier, fingering her hair or the bed sheets, but she never developed any firm attachment to a specific transitional object. According to Winnicott, the lack of a firm transitional-object attachment might be attributed to the lack of good-enough mothering, a view we certainly would not contest. However, the mother's offering of her own body in the transition to sleep tends in general, even where there is good-enough mothering, to militate against the investment of an inanimate object with mother-self significance. In this particular instance, where the mother's own capacity for object relatedness was so severely marred, both the adaptive and the pathological significance of her handling of her baby's falling to sleep are like two faces of the same coin. In view of her very limited capacity to establish for her baby a climate of strong emotional contact, the maximum tactile and kinesthetic closeness during the feeding situation at least tended to reinforce the sense of her presence in this important dyadic interaction; at the same time this same behavior, with its rigid insistence on body closeness, reflects her own uncertain sense of separateness and body-self integrity.

For Jody, then, with unstable core representations of self and object, the two-week separation at 13 months had a profound impact. Although the general outline of her responses — sleep and feeding disturbances, and an anxious hostile clinging — are what we would expect of a child this age, the intensity and the duration of the resonance of the experience are idiosyncratic, the result of the early strain in her development.

The unusual sleep disturbance and her other symptoms reflect the profound challenge of object loss with which this infant had to struggle in the aftermath of the separation experience. The inability of the mother to follow through, in spite of the initial success, on our suggestion for an alteration in the going-to-sleep routine reflects the mother's own disturbed capacity for separate functioning. The underlying rationale in our intervention was that allowing the child the possession of the bottle when she was put down in the crib alone would facilitate her investment of this inanimate object with mother-me significance and thus ease the transition to sleep which evokes a sense of self-dissolution and object loss.

A related and significant consequence of the separation was the intensification of object-directed hostile aggression. Even in the early, normal differentiation phase (Mahler and Furer, 1968), as the object is placed outside the area of omnipotent control, or, to put it another way, the object concept becomes external to the self-concept (Winnicott, 1969), there is an upsurge in object-directed aggression as a complement to the implicit object loss. In a situation of actual object loss such as a separation experience, the aggression is of course very much exaggerated. This was amply reflected in Jody's biting and other aggressive attacks on her mother, as well as on other people and inanimate objects. A particularly ominous aspect of the expansion of her hostile aggression was the early erotization of aggression, as reflected in the eruption of sharp teasing of the mother, and an unusually intense ambivalence, evidenced by the infant's affectionately hugging her mother and then suddenly biting her shoulder. Jody's observers were exposed to the same phenomenon: they knew something was coming, but could not tell until it actually occurred whether it would be a kiss or an attack.

A further reverberation of the separation experience was Jody's illness with a cold, temperature elevation, and diarrhea immediately after her parents' return. We have found that many of the children in our study developed some such illness in the first week after the parents' return from a separation of more than several days. We believe that the upsurge in aggression evoked by the separation experience is particularly disruptive to the establishment of the self and object representations. This upsurge of aggression seems to mobilize some somatization or, to follow Schur (1955, 1958), a resomatization, which is a precursor of defensive formation. This process may be a crucial mechanism in in-

fants of this age, since their libidinal attachment to the
object is still quite fragile and psychological defense
mechanisms that might be less compromising are not
yet available to them.

Jody had already shown some preliminary evidence of anal awareness when the separation experience
intensified her preoccupation with anal functions, particularly as a channel for expressing concerns about the
issues of object loss and self-dissolution. Perhaps the
most dramatic reflection of this anal channeling was the
growing anxiety she showed some three weeks after the
separation whenever her soiled diaper was changed. In-
terestingly, it was in this context that she began to hide
objects belonging to her mother. Her "Caca, dada, bye-
bye" vividly expressed the intimate relation of bowel
function with object-loss concerns. Most infants show a
marked reluctance to have their soiled diapers changed
sometime during the second year. The intensity of
Jody's anxiety and the fierceness of her resistance under-
scores her unusual concern about body integrity and the
threat of object loss. It seems that a period of time is required to detach from the stool its emotional significance of self and object.

It will be recalled that directly following her parents' return, Jody demonstrated the sexual arousal
typical of infants in the middle of the second year. Most
of the little girls we have studied displace their attention
from where the disturbing difference between the sexes
is to other areas, such as the umbilicus or the buttocks,
or to anal functions where the similarities are after all
more pronounced. Jody's curious and evocative verbalization, "Caca, dada, bye-bye" seems to betray the

important further concern about the lack of a penis —
that is, the stool has acquired the additional significance
of the father's phallus.

When Jody was about 14 months old, almost im-
perceptibly her mother's handling of the going-to-sleep
routine altered. While she continued to hold and rock
Jody, she increasingly patted her backside and held her
hand through the bars of the crib. At about this time we
learned, on speaking with the maternal grandmother,
that Jody's mother, whose own crib had always been in
the parental bedroom, also had a pacifier but no transitional object. The maternal grandmother had sat in a
straight-back chair and rocked her baby by rocking her
own body back and forth. After the father was taken
from the family, the mother had moved her daughter's
crib closer to her own bed and held her hand through its
bars. Jody's mother was as visibly startled to hear this
history as we were, since it so closely paralleled her own
handling of her baby's going to sleep. The shift in the
going-to-sleep ritual from the body-rocking to the hand-
holding took place when Jody was around 16 to 17
months, very close to Jody's mother's age when her own
father was taken away.

Between her 14th and 20th months, Jody was subjected to repeated separations from one or both parents
totaling about seven weeks in all. The separations
ranged in duration from one day to two weeks. Although the mother had some awareness of how disruptive these experiences were for her daughter, both
parents allowed themselves to be driven by what they
thought were the realities of their situation. No sooner

would this sturdy little girl show some signs of mastering one separation experience than she would be confronted with another. Although Jody never again
showed the massive acute sleep disturbance in response
to the subsequent separations that she showed at 13
months, there was no period of time when her sleep was
undisturbed.

Increasing incursions into her developing object relations with her father and her autonomy resulted from
each subsequent separation. At first Jody rushed into her
mother's arms in happy reunion but invariably ignored
her father for varying periods of time. After a three-day
separation at about 15 months, she was quite frightened
when she was approached by men, particularly strange
men for about two days: she averted her eyes and rushed
to her mother for comfort. At 17 months, after a two-
week separation, in addition to ignoring her father for
two days, she developed a highly unusual confusion in
names, calling her father by her grandfather's name
and referring to her grandfather as "dada." At 18
months, after a five-day separation, after initially showing some fear of her father on reunion, the anxiety was
displaced and instead she was afraid of noises, rolling
balls, and shadows for two weeks. At 19½ months,
after her mother was away for five days and her father
for two weeks, she again seemed frightened of her
father for several days. Shortly after this she was heard
to repeat to herself, "Mama, dada, Jody, family." At 20
months, after an overnight separation, she said to her
parents, "Jody has two mommies and two daddies." It
had been her mother's custom, in an effort to reassure
Jody, to say to Jody either before or after separation,

"Mommie sometimes goes away but she always comes back." Just shortly before the nursery discontinued, Jody was heard to utter the pathetic and plaintive reply, "Mommie always goes away."

Each of these many separations was followed by a gradually extended period of anxious clinging to her mother. Jody now intently watched the activities of others, rather than directly engaging herself with them or initiating activity herself. In this connection a poignant play sequence observed at home was very much to the point. Instead of the playful and pleasurable spoon-feeding of her doll's mouth which she had often engaged in before, she now rather sober-facedly spoon-fed her doll's eyes. Her vision had assumed an oral-incorporative quality. Her growing constriction in self-initiated play became so extreme that there was no organized activity unless she was at her mother's side and was urged to play.

From age 15 months Jody, with her "Jody, mama, gina, Dada, penis" made a clear verbal distinction between male and female. She now was reported to notice her mother's tampons, and tried to pull on the tampon string. She insisted on having a tampon of her own, which she tried to insert in her genitals. The mother insisted that Jody had never seen a bloody tampon. At this time her favorite activity was the rocking horse, which she would ride vigorously. At 17 months she clutched at her father's penis and pubic hair in the bathtub and was reported to insist with glee, "I'm a boy." For some time after, she sat on the floor with her legs apart and placed various toys between her legs. Toward the end of her 18th month there was a sharp falling off of genital manipulation; she no longer named either penis or vagina, and for some time she stopped looking at and touching her father's penis. She also showed increased curiosity about her belly button which she would occasionally rub for long periods of time and so intensively that the whole area became painful; she then discontinued this activity. At 18 months she frequently clutched her genital area whenever she was frightened. Shortly after the umbilical masturbatory activity ceased, she repeatedly stuffed tissues and other objects into her blouse, proudly showing her breasts, and was increasingly interested in the breasts of her mother and her female observers, frequently pinching them suddenly.

Clearly the central experience with which Jody had to struggle was the essential unavailability of her mother, whether it was the emotional unavailability in her early months or her actual unavailability in the second year.

While Jody's mother was distinctly aware of how disruptive separations were for her daughter, a quick, easy denial would overtake this margin of awareness as she ascribed Jody's disturbance to what seemed like endless teething, colds, her age, etc. The frequent separations seem to reflect the mother's compulsion to repeat with her daughter her own traumatic past.

An interesting and significant idiosyncratic detail of Jody's behavior on her parents' return after a separation was her immediate and joyous reunion with her mother and her tendency to ignore her father beginning with the separation when she was 17 months old. Ordinarily, after a separation from the parents during the second year of life, the child ignores the mother and rushes to the father, since the aggression mobilized by separation is directed at the mother. The father, who is increasingly utilized by the child as the supporting separator in the separation-individuation process away from the mother (Mahler and Gosliner, 1955; Greenacre, 1966; Abelin, 1971) ordinarily is spared the anger. We assume that the central imperative in Jody's functioning was to spare and bolster her relationship with her mother at whatever cost because of the early disturbance in their attachment. When Jody was reunited with her parents, it was toward the father of separation that the rage was directed, albeit this trend would serve to disturb her development toward ultimate independence and a later positive oedipal attachment to the father.

These mechanisms were only partially able to blunt the rage toward the mother. Only a few days after each separation, her hostility would ultimately find its primary target, her mother, as she directed toward her the biting, pinching, slapping attacks. Moreover, over time there was, as we have said, an ever-increasing sadomasochistic erotization of their relationship, reflected in the increasingly prominent teasing behavior between them.

In the highly important area of drive organization during the second year, the anal and early sexual zonal thrusts were concomitantly, almost from the beginning, caught up in pronounced conflict. Instead of serving to support and consolidate Jody's developing self and object representations as they normally would, the conflict in these areas further undermined and depleted these developments.

The normally occurring early sexual-zone arousal opens a new channel for the consolidation of the libidinal attachment to the object and of a primary genital outline of the body, a central peg in the infant's developing sexual identity. Although Jody's masturbatory arousal from her 13th to 18th months was relatively normal in its increasing intensity, we were from very early on impressed that, unlike most other children, she showed very little pleasure when she touched her genitals. We believe that the virtual absence of masturbatory pleasure was due to the contamination of Jody's libidinal attachment by very strong currents of hostile aggression, as reflected in the unusually pronounced ambivalence and the early, intense erotization of aggression.

In summary, the considerable disturbance in the mother-child interaction led to a much greater-than-ordinary aggressive contamination of libidinal currents. With the emergence of the normal sexual arousal in the middle of the second year, Jody's masturbatory activity was relatively without masturbatory pleasure in contrast to the normally developing child whose pleasure in masturbation seems to expand and fortify the sense of self and sexual identity. Her penis envy led to a brief period of denial of the difference, a denial that was unsuccessful and was followed by an inhibition of genital activity and displacement to the umbilicus. But this masturbatory variant was so contaminated with hostile aggression that it ultimately led to self-injury and was followed, at least for a time, by a total inhibition of masturbation, interfering with her developing sense of sexual identity. We then saw the re-emergence of a reinforced denial through the fantasy of the displaced breast-phallus and what might be called a fetishistic attachment (see Chapter 10) to the menstrual tampon. With all this, we have seen the virtual drying up and depletion of that important libidinal wellspring, the early sexual zone thrust, and a still further accretion to that defensive bulwark which served bravely but in pyrrhic fashion to preserve the precarious sense of self and object.

CHAPTER 9

THE TRANSITIONAL OBJECT

Ever since Winnicott's (1953) description of transitional phenomena and the familiar objects around which they usually center, and especially in the past decade, the focus on the various attributes and vicissitudes of these phenomena has been increasing. Indeed, Winnicott's ideas have had such explanatory power in connection with the infant's developing sense of self and object, symbolic thought, and reality orientation that it has almost seemed as if we have always known them. Winnicott suggested that the child's first possession is related to past autoerotic phenomena and also to future playthings like the first soft animal or doll. It is related to both the external object (mother's breast) and to the internal object (the magically introjected breast) but is distinct from each.

Winnicott introduced the terms transitional objects and transitional phenomena as designations for an intermediate area of experience which he conceived of as existing between the thumb and the doll, between oral erotism and true object relatedness, between primary creativeness and objective perception based on reality testing. This early stage in development is made possible by the mother's special capacity for adapting to her infant's needs, thus allowing the infant the illusion that what he or she creates really exists. This intermediate area of experience, belonging exactly to neither internal nor external shared reality, constitutes a significant part of the infant's experience. Throughout life it is retained, according to Winnicott, in the intense experience that belongs to religion, mythology, the arts, and shared belief systems. The transitional object plays a central and flexible role as the infant copes with ordinary and normal strains implicit in the attainment of upright mobility (Greenacre, 1969, 1970), the separation-individuation phase (Mahler, 1963, 1967; Mahler and Furer, 1968; Mahler et al., 1975), and the anal-urinary and early genital stages of development. Each of these strains provokes a greater or lesser degree of anxiety about both object loss and self-dissolution. As Winnicott has pointed out, the transitional object or transitional phenomena tend to blur a threatening sense of separateness. They thus become vitally important to the infant at the time of going to sleep and as a defense against anxiety, especially that of threatened object loss. Patterns set in infancy may persist into childhood; the original soft object may continue to be absolutely necessary at bedtime, or at times of loneliness, frustration, injury, or when a depressive mood threatens. In health, however, there is gradually an extension in the range of interest, and eventually the extended range is maintained even when object-loss anxiety threatens. In this chapter we report the direct observations of the behavior of one of our research infants to demonstrate the rich patterns ordinarily displayed by babies in their use of the first not-me possession in the context of maturing ego and drive development.

SARAH

Sarah, the infant to be described, was a first-born whose delivery and early development were normal and of good quality except for severe colic which plagued her during the first five months. As a result of the colic the usual cycles of hunger arousal, feeding, satiation, and sleep were not established early. Instead, the feeding which stilled the pangs of hunger also led to marked intestinal distress with cramping and gas pains. The mother had to hold, walk, and rock her infant for relatively long periods of time in order that she might be comforted sufficiently to fall asleep.

With the resolution of the colic, Sarah became a good sleeper, hearty eater, and a cheerful, sturdy baby. When she entered the nursery at 11 months she was a vigorous and rapid crawler. Like most of the babies when confronted by the many strangers in the nursery, Sarah tended to cling to her mother and spent most of the first morning either in her mother's lap or on the floor at her feet. Unlike the other babies, that first morning Sarah selected, out of the whole array of blocks, nesting toys, stuffed animals, dolls, trucks, and balls, a Raggedy Ann doll to which she clung tenaciously until it was time to leave. She had an identical Raggedy Ann doll at home, in which she had heretofore shown no particular interest. Within the first five minutes of each subsequent morning at the nursery, she staked out her claim to the doll, clinging to it the entire time and passionately defending her claim to it against any other child. Within a day or two the doll was almost constantly in her hand at home too, and she soon required Raggedy Ann in her crib on going to sleep. Apart from this clinging pattern of play with Raggedy Ann, Sarah showed no discernible organized pattern of play with it. After a few weeks, however, when her mother awakened her from sleep, Sarah would hand her the doll before allowing herself to be taken from the crib. During the same period, both at home and at the nursery, Sarah was frequently observed to affectionately hug and kiss her doll—some three months before she displayed the same affectionate behavior with her mother.

As with most of the infants, Sarah's range of interest and activity gradually extended from the narrow physical orbit of her mother. She was observed to crawl vigorously around the nursery, dragging Raggedy Ann along with her, spending longer and longer spans of time away from her mother, stopping here and there to scatter, bang, and throw toys. From her 12th to 13th month she began to walk with support, steadying herself by pushing a chair or carriage. By 13 months she was standing unaided, and over the next several weeks she became a secure toddler. During the period when she was using chairs and the carriage to aid her walking, Sarah was usually observed to place the Raggedy Ann on the chair or in the carriage. On one such occasion, when pushing the carriage, she tentatively let go and after a few seconds of free standing, collapsed. She raised herself, very deliberately took the Raggedy Ann out of the carriage, dropped it on the floor, then picked it up, hugged it, and gently replaced it in the carriage. Holding on to the carriage, she walked on.

Sarah's response to the strange nursery was unique in that it led to her attachment to a transitional object, the Raggedy Ann doll. She conforms here to Winnicott's descriptions in that her attachment to the transitional object was precipitated as a defense against separation and stranger anxiety. It readily served as a bridge between the unfamiliar nursery setting and the constant setting of the crib, inasmuch as the same doll was present in both places. However, the intense and meaningful attachment to the doll was her own creative act. That is, the infant through its projection onto the inanimate object of the mother-me significance animates the doll in the process, and it can serve to comfort the infant through its tendency to blur the sense of separateness. Sperling (1963) seemed to think that the mother is important in the choice of the transitional object. With Winnicott, we do not agree; we think the infant chooses and animates the inanimate object — and that this animation is the prototype of creativity, as in the Pygmalion myth. The Raggedy Ann soon became obligatory in the paradigmatic situation of object loss, falling asleep. Like other children, Sarah experienced a painful giving up of her mother on going to sleep and utilized the transitional object as a reassuring and comforting indication of her mother's presence.

While Sarah, in time, developed rich and elaborate semisymbolic play with the transitional-object doll, her simple holding, clinging contact with it, particularly when she was anxious, persisted.

It is curious that this youngster, unlike most infants, chose a doll for her first transitional object, rather than the more ubiquitous blanket. We wonder whether the early colic may not have been implicated in this choice. It is generally thought that the repeated pattern of need arousal and satiation forms the nucleus around which the infant ultimately consolidates some reliable indication of the external real object world. Where feeding results in distress, as it does with colic, we think that there must be a resultant instability in the developing self and object representations. It is tempting to speculate that it may have been precisely as a result of this instability that Sarah chose to invest the doll, because of its similarity in form and configuration to the human figure, rather than choosing an amorphous blanket.

The significance of the attachment to the transitional object in the initiation of an affectionate type of object relationship was clearly demonstrated in Sarah's tender hugging and kissing of her Raggedy Ann some three months before similar behavior with her own mother. Does this, as Sperling (1963) asserted, reflect a pathological turning to an inanimate object in preference to the real, live object? To the contrary, in Sarah's case her affectionate behavior toward her Raggedy Ann involved a predominantly active relationship to the object. That is, it was held, comforted, kissed, whereas her relationship with her own mother, while undergoing rapid changes, was still predominantly a passive-dependent one. Indeed, when Sarah first came to the nursery, her selection and attachment to an already familiar Raggedy Ann reflected the nucleus of active stirrings of mastery. Is this not precisely the progressive, wholesome aspect of the child's attachment to the transitional object? It seems to us that such a development facilitates and serves to consolidate active trends of the self in relation to the object in the face of a major and still powerful passive-dependent relationship to the mother. The significance of active patterns in relation to the transitional object was touchingly indicated when Sarah, after having herself fallen, deliberately dropped her Raggedy Ann and then affectionately hugged her. What clearer instance could be found of actively repeating with the doll what she had passively experienced?

It is just this duality — active-independent strivings versus a still powerful passive-dependent attachment to the mother — which Mahler (1963, 1967) has so well described in connection with the separation-individuation phase. A consideration of some of the foregoing descriptions of Sarah, feeding herself, resisting the passivity of being dressed or diapered, etc., will underscore the determination with which this little girl seemed to defend her nascent and still shaky active self.

Greenacre (1970), in her discussion of the role of the transitional object, has emphasized a somewhat different but related consideration, stating, ". . . a normal period of increased strain in the healthy and 'good'-mothered infant occurs toward the latter part of the first year and the first half of the second, when both speech and bipedal locomotion are being established simultaneously with rapid growth in body size and general functioning. . . . The transitional object serves as a faithful protective escort, when needed, in this exciting and sometimes uncertain time" (p. 342).

From her 13th through her 14th month, Sarah's push toward individuation took on a more rapid pace. She now insisted on feeding herself and showed clear and decided interests in some foods as against others. She resisted diapering and being dressed. Her anger, now for the first time easily recognizable as such, became sharper and more object directed. For example, when frustrated by her mother's removing a toy from her, Sarah would arch her back, scream, and crawl away rapidly into another room, slapping her hands hard on the floor. Waking at night, an infrequent occurrence before this time, increased particularly on those nights when Sarah was left with a babysitter. Now, too, anal awareness and the first tentative genital touching were observed, and peek-a-boo games became very frequent. In addition to clinging to Raggedy Ann, Sarah would rock the doll on the rocking horse (her favorite activity), brush its hair, and after each meal place it in her high chair and pretend to feed it.

Early one evening, when Sarah was 14 months old, her father came into the bathroom and urinated while she was having her bath. Whereas this had happened occasionally in the first year, it had not occurred, to the best of her mother's memory, in the preceding four or five months. Sarah stared fixedly and then began to giggle. The father, noting her response, told his wife he would avoid exposing himself in front of her in the future. But in spite of the resolution, he continued to expose himself with some regularity while showering or urinating over the next seven months, as far as we knew.

Sarah slept poorly that night, waking several times, and a fair degree of sleep disturbance occurred over the following three months.

The next morning, at the nursery, Sarah watched intently a somewhat older boy straddling a wooden toy train and pushing it along. As soon as he had left the train, she succeeded, with some difficulty, in straddling it. She then lifted the toy train cover, stuffed her Raggedy Ann in the bin, covered it, and straddled the train once more, rolling it back and forth with a dreamy, inwardly directed gaze. This became a favorite activity, repeated over and over. We were impressed by the repetition of the intent and fixed staring, which had characterized the earlier exposure experience with the father. Could the special appeal of Sarah's activity have been that she recognized that the male child had something between his legs? By her touchingly clumsy enactment of this same activity, rocking back and forth on the toy train in a dreamy and detached attitude, she too could support for a while the feeling fantasy that she also had that "something." However, as if this were not sufficient to bolster the illusion, she attempted to re-enforce it by stuffing her Raggedy Ann, with all its emotional fullness of "mother-me," into the bin before straddling it.

Sarah now also watched intently as her mother urinated on the toilet. When her mother put the lid down, Sarah raised it and attempted to dip her Raggedy Ann's head into the bowl. Her mother restrained her. However, several times over the next several weeks, both at home and in the nursery, Sarah emerged from the bathroom with Raggedy Ann's hair dripping wet.

We think the dangling of her Raggedy Ann represented a condensation of interests in the mother's pubic hair, the urinary stream, and the renewed assertion of the mother-me dyad. Her intent observation of her mother during urination established a difference between mother and herself, as well as a similarity between mother and father — the existence of pubic hair. Sarah bravely attempted to bridge that difference when she repetitively and triumphantly emerged from the bathroom with her own Raggedy Ann, its curly, kinky hair dripping, thus supporting the illusion that she also had pubic hair.

Actually, Sarah had for many months been accustomed to being in the bathroom when her mother used the toilet, but before the occasion mentioned above, had not paid any attention to her mother's toilet functions or pubic area. Over the next several months, however, she showed an intense visual and tactile curiosity about her mother's pubic hair, genitals, umbilicus, and breasts. She also compared her own anatomy with that of both her mother and father whenever they were exposed. From this time her genital self-stimulation increased in frequency and intensity. Later, the frequent inspection and comparison of the genital anatomy came to extend to a comparison of teeth, nose, eyes, and ears of mother, father, and self.

On subsequent occasions, when she saw her father's penis, Sarah got her Raggedy Ann, pulled its pants down, conspicuously examining it between the legs; she would then go to her mother, pull her robe open, point to the pubic hair and say, "Gina." The transitional-object doll, which served as a bridge in this sequence, seemed to lend a versatile illusionary support to a new variety of experience — the troubling confrontation with the anatomical difference between the sexes — by relating the experience back to earlier ones when contact with the mother was more constant and assured.

Gradually over the next several weeks, she began to extend the passionate involvement with Raggedy Ann to a whole collection of dolls and stuffed animals. She similarly began to examine them between the legs. On a few occasions, with a stuffed rabbit or a doll, she pointed and said, "Belly button," although none was there.

While Sarah continued to carry her Raggedy Ann around, her play became increasingly elaborate. She developed an astonishing variety of peek-a-boo games with the Raggedy Ann and later with her other dolls. She discovered how to open and close drawers and incessantly stuffed the doll into the drawer and then found it again. She would put the doll into a room, close the door, and then opening it would affectionately hug the doll. On a number of occasions, in the midst of this repetitive play, Sarah placed Raggedy Ann between her legs and held it there for some time. She also developed a great interest in the jack-in-the-box and in placing pegs into and through holes.

In addition to all this play with Raggedy Ann, which seemed so decisively related to her genital curiosity, Sarah also developed an elaborate variety of symbolic games with her doll, which included dressing and undressing, putting her to bed, wheeling her in a carriage, pretending feeding and rocking, etc. It should be noted that, along with the somewhat precocious symbolic play with the dolls, she continued a good part of the time, both at home and in the nursery, to simply cling to Raggedy Ann, whatever else she might be doing.

The interesting and elaborate play patterns that emerged with the transitional-object doll give us the most evocative indications of the underlying dynamic resonance of the whole experience in this little girl. The repetitive explorations paralleled the continued exploration of self, mother, and father, and not only reflected the need to establish and re-enforce the perceptual outlines of the experience but also indicated the enormous difficulty Sarah had in integrating the genital outline of her body, a development so central to the infant's emerging sense of sexual identity.

Sarah, as has been noted, had already achieved anal awareness when she first perceived her father's penis. She was also regularly and correctly using the word "doody" when she had a movement. Over the next month or so, although her mother had as yet made no effort at toilet training, Sarah was observed crouching while she had her bowel movements. She would also leave the room, if her mother was present, before having the movement. By 15 months, a high level of sphincter control was already established. For example, she might be in the car with her mother, begin to squirm and say "Doody," but wait until they returned home some 20 minutes later before crouching and having her bowel movement. From this time on she tended to have her movements exclusively during her waking hours while she was wearing a diaper, and only when she was left with a babysitter did she have a bowel movement at night during her sleep. She stringently resisted having her soiled diapers changed and on occasions would fiercely pull her mother's hair.

Behavior related to urinary functions changed as well. About two days after she had first seen her father urinate, in the midst of pleasurable play during bath time, Sarah suddenly stood up and urinated. From this time on, whenever she was undressed in preparation for her bath, she would urinate on the floor, sometimes bending over to watch. Soon she began to say the word "cissy" in anticipation. At 16 months, her mother got her a potty and said, "Don't make cissy on the floor, use the pot," and with this placed Sarah on the pot. Sarah angrily got up, stuffed the Raggedy Ann in the bowl and slammed the lid. She invariably squirmed and cried when her mother placed her on the pot. But she often sat down on the potty herself, fully clothed. On a number of occasions she stuffed Raggedy Ann and one or two other favorite dolls into the bowl and sat on top of them contentedly for a long time. Once, when she was around 17 months, her mother surprised her in the act, and Sarah, rather startled, urinated in the pot. After this she no longer urinated on the floor before bath time, doing it instead in the bath or in her diaper. At about this time she developed some verbal confusion in naming urination and bowel movements, whereas heretofore she had consistently named them correctly. She also began to point to her mother's, father's, and her own umbilicus and say "Cissy," whereas she had always correctly named the navel before.

Sarah's response to the exposure over the next three months was dramatic indeed. The direct stimulating effect of the exposure was reflected in the abrupt intensification of her genital self-stimulation, which over the next several months developed into a distinct masturbatory pattern. The immediate upsurge after the exposure does seem to point to the provocative and organizing role it played in Sarah's particular experience. The perception of the anatomical difference, coming after signs of early genital arousal, seemed to mobilize a castration reaction.

Not until Sarah was between 17 and 18 months did her direct sexual curiosity about the similarities and differences in her mother's, father's, and her own sexual anatomy abate. But even then the preoccupation with the comparisons of the umbilicus, mouth, nose, eyes, and ears continued, reflecting a displacement of genital concerns. It seems probable, too, that the confusion in naming bowel and bladder functions that arose simultaneously also reflected a displaced disturbance about the genital difference. At the same time the still powerful underlying confusion led to a deterioration of the hard-won bowel and bladder self-awareness.

By rushing Raggedy Ann into the gap created by the observation of the difference between the father on the one hand, and mother and self, on the other (that is, the presence of the phallus), Sarah not only attempted to repair the rent in the body-self integrity, but also to cope with the complementary disturbance produced by this observation — the rise in object-loss anxiety. She seemed to react to the difference as if it were a loss, a loss of a sense of completeness, which to a child of this age has the meaning of a loss of the emotional availability of the mother. The intensification of the object-loss anxiety was reflected in the emergence once again of a sleep disturbance. The transitional-object doll was ideally suited as a bridge in this situation since it tended to alter the sharp and threatening sense of separateness and re-enforced the reassuring "mother-me" dyadic relationship. It is noteworthy that at just this time an alteration in the "going-to-sleep" ritual took place. No longer was it sufficient to have her transitional-object doll close at hand when she fell off to sleep alone in her crib. She now fell asleep lying prone on top of her doll, which not only offered a more certain sense of the object's presence but, by its very position, offered the comforting illusion of phallic completeness. The doll stood for the missing penis and in this fashion seemed to lay the groundwork for a rudimentary fantasy of the body-phallus equation.

Normally, the sexual arousal that is characteristic of the second year concerns itself with the expansion and consolidation of the sense of self and object. At this juncture of development, the castration anxiety converges with and is indissoluble from the anxieties of object loss and self-annihilation; we do not find one without some resonance on the other plane. In the phallic phase, with the further solidification and constancy of the self and object representations, the castration fear, powerful and organizing as it may be, no longer carries the immediate, more global meaning of threatened object loss and self-annihilation as is the case in the early stage of sexual development.

We believe the foregoing discussion demonstrates that at this stage in development an experience that confronted Sarah with the anatomical difference between the sexes had a major dynamic impact on the stage-specific planes of object loss and self-dissolution.

Sarah's behavior indicated the close connection between her bowel movements and her relation with the maternal object, including the general need to re-establish the mother's emotional availability. Only when her mother left her did Sarah deposit and separate from the "stool-mother" — angrily, we would suppose — without paying the slightest attention to it: she had the bowel movement while asleep, apparently paying no attention to its loss.

Sarah's attention to her own urination as well as that of her mother and father continued at a high level of intensity for some time after she first saw her father's penis, as evidenced by her consistently urinating on the floor whenever undressed for a bath, and bending over and watching the stream and where it came from. This pattern of bowel and bladder awareness, emerging early in the second year, is usual in most of the children we have observed and entirely independent of any toilet-training efforts. It seems to be related to the increasing organization of body-self awareness and object relatedness. Training efforts are complicated by the fears of body-self loss and object loss which are typical for children of this age. We saw that when Sarah's mother mildly urged her to use a pot, she angrily stuffed her Raggedy Ann in the bowl and shut the lid, that she also stuffed the bowl with several of her precious dolls and sat contentedly, fully clothed, on the pot for long periods of time. The use of the pot to give up stool and urine provokes so much resistance and anxiety precisely because these products are invested with the emotionally laden significance of self and object.

At 18 months, Sarah's parents took a one-week vacation, leaving her with her maternal grandparents. This was the first time the parents had left Sarah for more than a day. During this week, she seemed warm and affectionate with her grandparents but at the same time remarkably sober and subdued. Her sleep, which in the two or three weeks before the separation had improved considerably, again became disturbed, and she awoke three or four times a night.

When her parents returned she all but ignored her mother for 24 hours, but immediately and joyfully rushed into her father's arms, hugging and kissing him. Almost immediately after the reunion a new variety of peek-a-boo games developed. She endlessly covered and then uncovered her Raggedy Ann and other dolls with a towel or blanket, and affectionately hugged them on reunion. The day after her parents returned, while having a diaper changed, she put her Raggedy Ann doll directly to her genitals and said "Cissy." Shortly after this, while her father was sitting in a robe, talking on the telephone, Sarah, who may possibly have seen his penis exposed, kept pointing and repeating the word "penis" over and over again. Then she looked down at her pubic area and said, "Sarah, penis." Although this had been implicit in her behavior before, it was the first time that she explicitly stated that she had a "penis."

Four days after her parents returned, they took Sarah on a week's trip with an aunt and uncle and their son and daughter. From the onset, Sarah was unusually anxious and clinging, barely able to tolerate being out of her parents' sight. Once during the trip, when looking at her father's penis, she said "Mine." Her mother, uncertain about her meanng since there was still the age-appropriate confusion of "mine" and "yours," said "Daddy's penis." Sarah replied in no uncertain terms, "Sarah's penis."

During the trip, and for the first time, she became unusually sensitive to minor cuts and bruises and insisted that her parents repeatedly kiss the injured part. With her boy cousin, she developed a game which she played with him over and over again: she would take some possession away from him and then with considerable pleasure return it to him; in reverse he would then take something of hers and she would gleefully retrieve it. She frequently placed her Raggedy Ann on the pot and then sat on top of the doll. She incessantly diapered and undiapered all of her dolls, and placed them on the pot.

After returning from the trip, Sarah continued to be cranky and clinging and within a few days developed chicken pox which centered in the perineal area. The itching increased her irritability so that her tolerance for frustration was minimal. She seemed almost constantly to be in a "temper" and, for a while, was so beside herself that she banged her head against the wall. During the week following her return, when her irritability was at its height, she completely ignored her Raggedy Ann.

Over the next few months, Sarah's masturbation continued at a high level of intensity and frequency. She insisted that she had a penis and often said that her dolls and her mother also had one. Once, looking at her father's nipples, she correctly named them; then looking at his umbilicus, she said, "Daddy, gina."

We attribute the intensity of Sarah's castration reaction, more than three months after her initial exposure to the anatomical difference, to the anxiety and rage produced by the combination of events in her 18th month. The week-long separation from her parents, followed almost immediately by the trip to strange lands, intensified her castration anxiety. It is even possible that some of her aggression took the somatic form of chicken pox (see Chapter 8). But the most eloquent evidence for the close association between castration anxiety and object-loss anxiety was in Sarah's altered relationship to her Raggedy Ann.

Shortly after returning from the trip, Sarah became very attached to a toy wooden bull her parents had bought as a souvenir of their trip. She played with it constantly, took it to bed, and frequently brought it to the nursery. Unable to tolerate any other child's playing with it, she would place it in her mother's purse. Her attachment to the bull over the next two months overshadowed and all but displaced her interest in Raggedy Ann and the other dolls.

From the beginning she tugged at the bull's penis and, of course, because the toy penis was constructed as a peg in a hole, the penis came off. Sarah was startled and delighted and continued to pull it off and have her mother put it back. She kissed, mouthed, and bit the penis, threw it on the floor, vigorously kicked it about, and then affectionately said, "Nice penis." At the same time her own genital manipulation, with its vigorous pinching of the labia, often had an aggressive quality. From time to time a sharp teasing emerged in relation to her mother. This was particularly notable in her continued insistence that she had a penis or that she was a boy. Sarah did not fail to notice that this distressed her mother, who empathically felt the narcissistic insult. It was at this time that she frequently was heard to say, on seeing her father exposed, "Nice penis." In her 20th month, reports continued of Sarah falling and scraping a knee or merely bruising it. These accidents uniformly provoked profound crying with obvious anxiety entirely disproportionate to the nature of the injury. She would cling to her mother and frequently insist on being carried for some time. She would actually favor the injured member by limping for an hour or two afterward.

Sarah's preoccupation with toilet functions continued at a very high level. By this time she readily sat on the pot, but success was rare. On one occasion, while sitting on the pot she urinated; although usually highly verbal, she said nothing. When her mother gave her some toilet tissue to wipe herself, she did so for a very long time, then said, "Sarah wipes penis."

CHAPTER 10

THE INFANTILE FETISH

Fetishism, one of the most bizarre and florid perversions of the human sexual instinct, has attracted the attention of many psychoanalytic and psychiatric investigators. The fetish is an inanimate object which is adopted as a necessary prop to insure adequate sexual performance in adult life. Tracing the development of adult fetishists in psychoanalysis, Gillespie (1952), Bak (1953, 1968), and Greenacre (1970) found that the fetish first emerges in the phallic phase and during latency.

Any discussion of the genetic and dynamic roots of fetishism must start with Freud's original contributions to this topic, which occupied him over a period of 35 years. In 1905 Freud described fetishism as an "unsuitable substitute for the sexual object." He stated: "What is substituted for the [normal] sexual object is some part of the body... which is in general very inappropriate for sexual purposes, or an inanimate object which bears an assignable relation to the person whom it replaces" (p. 153).

189

He wrote that a certain degree of fetishism is normal and ubiquitous, as in the overevaluation of the love object which inevitably extends to everything associated with the beloved. The condition becomes pathological only in those cases in which the fetish replaces the normal object. He also alluded to intermediary states in which the sexual partner must have certain distinct qualities, a particular hair coloring, for example.

In footnotes added to later editions of "Three Essays," just quoted, Freud further extended our understanding of fetishism. In 1910 he pointed to the importance of the coprophilic pleasure in smelling as one determinant in the choice of the fetish and alluded to the role of the castration complex in fetishism: "Another factor that helps towards explaining the fetishistic preference for the foot is to be found among the sexual theories of children: the foot represents a woman's penis, the absence of which is deeply felt" (p. 155). Freud emphasized the central and organizing role of the castration complex in the precipitation of fetishism in his definitive paper on fetishism (1927), in which he offered several additional considerations. He asserted that the fetish becomes the vehicle for both denying and affirming the fact of castration and in this manner brings about a split in the ego, a point he further elaborated in 1938. In addition, he wrote: "Affection and hostility in the treatment of the fetish — which run parallel with the disavowal and the acknowledgment of castration — are mixed in unequal proportions in different cases, so that one or the other is more clearly recognizable" (1927, p. 157).

A number of other authors, while recognizing the

organizing role of the castration complex in the structure of fetishism, have tended to emphasize the pre-oedipal threads in the fabric of the fetish. Abraham (1910) stressed the importance of sadomasochistic elements in the fetishist. The patient he described had a tendency to retain his excreta and had a lifelong fantasy in which he was forced to refrain from relieving either bowel or bladder. Bak (1953) described a patient whose relation to his fetish contained currents that condensed the tactile sensation of his mother's skin, her body smell, the smell of feces, and an illusory phallus.

In a series of papers on fetishism, Greenacre (1953a, 1955, 1960) emphasized a specific combination of genetic influences. She pointed to disturbances in the first 18 months of life which produce an instability in the formation of the body image, lead to uncertainty of the outline of the body, and fluctuations in the subjective sense of size, and, by bringing about complementary disturbances in the phallic phase, result in an exaggeration of the castration complex. Greenacre stressed that the infant has more difficulty in defining the genital area than most other parts of the body. Under normal conditions, she states, the genital schematization becomes consolidated during the phallic phase, due to an increase in the spontaneous endogenous sensations arising at that time. But where disturbances occur in the pregenital phase, such as a mother who is not good enough or an infant so impaired by injury, illness, or congenital defect that no mother can be good enough, the overly strong castration anxiety of the phallic phase is combined with the body-disintegration anxiety from the earlier phases and depletes rather than reinforces the genital schematization.

This brief review of the literature on adult fetishism serves to underline the main thematic outlines in the
precipitation of the fetish during the phallic phase or
during latency. An unusually sharp castration complex
is generally agreed to be the central organizing nucleus
in the structure of fetishism; this development occurs as
a result of severe disturbances in the areas of preoedipal
libidinal and aggressive drive economy, object relations,
and body-self schematization. Due to early disturbances
in the mother-infant relation, there is a severe impair-
ment of object relatedness which combines with an instability of the body-self image, especially with respect
to the genitals. This becomes most significant during the
phallic-oedipal period when castration anxiety is particularly acute as a result of the sharp aggression aroused
at this time. Recurring castration panic then ensues, for
which the fetish serves as a stopgap, permitting some
stabilization of the genital outline of the body image.

Greenacre later (1960, 1969, 1970) pointed to
fetishistic phenomena in which the "fetish" is not related
specifically to genital sexual performance. This conceptual extension offers the possibility of understanding a
wide range of individual and cultural practices, as well
as fetishisticlike phenomena in children which may be
the forerunners of adult fetishism.

Wulff (1946) presented observational vignettes of
phenomena which he termed infantile fetishism. Two
of the five cases he reported were seen by himself and
three were observed by colleagues.

The first case Wulff described was that of a boy a
little over four years old. When this youngster had a

pain or was in a bad humor or could not tolerate his mother's leaving, he had only to be given his "magic blanket"; he would then wrap his head in it and fall asleep peacefully and happily. Ever since he had been weaned from the breast he had prized this warm, soft coverlet more than anything in the world. Wulff's second case was that of a boy who was not quite two years old when he was separated from his mother and admitted to an orphanage. He became inseparably attached to his chamber pot and readily complied with the most difficult and disagreeable demands of upbringing so long as he was allowed to keep his pot, the most precious object in his world.

The first of Wulff's colleague's cases was that of a little girl who clung tenaciously and lovingly to a drooling bib which she had worn when she suckled at the breast. Since being weaned at six and a half months she would press this drooling cloth against her cheek and suck her thumb, contentedly falling asleep. It was her comforter and her protector when she was hurt, when something was taken from her, or when she was in a strange environment. Another case was a little boy, aged 15 months, who showed a special interest in a particular feeding bib. Whenever he went to bed, he took this bib, smelled it, and sucked it; under no circumstances would he be parted from it. When he was two and a half years old this bib disappeared, and for some time thereafter he was in low spirits and had great difficulty in falling asleep. He refused to accept a substitute and promptly became a regular bed-wetter. At the age of four, he became attached to his mother's handkerchiefs, whereupon he stopped wetting the bed. While he did not insist on a specific handkerchief, it had to have some residual odor of his mother's eau-de-cologne. He often stuffed it in his pajamas, holding it pressed against his penis, saying that in this way it could not get lost.

Finally, was the case of a little boy who during the first year of his life was accustomed to fall asleep with his mother's warm nightgown pressed between his hands, thumb in his mouth. At some point in the second year he began to prefer a brassiere or stocking which his mother had used.

Wulff calls each of these special infantile objects a fetish, clearly implying that they are for the infant a necessary aspect of the object which stands for the mother and her nurturing function. It seems to us that such terminology lacks conceptual clarity and is ambiguous in that it fails to demonstrate any genetic and dynamic continuity with the fetish of the phallic phase and of the adult perversion, at the core of which, virtually all investigators agree, the castration complex is the organizing nucleus.

In the cases of the drooling cloth, the feeding bib, and the magic blanket, Winnicott's (1953) concept of transitional objects, with its emphasis on the normal, healthy, and ubiquitous nature of this infantile construct, seems a much more appropriate one and avoids the ambiguity of Wulff's explanations. In the case of the two-year-old boy and his chamber pot, we lack sufficient developmental data to make a reasonable decision about the meaning of the behavior. On the other hand, the boy who used the handkerchief offers a clear instance of fetish formation in a four- to five-year-old, but this does not help us to answer the question whether an infantile fetish might make its appearance earlier than the phallic phase.

We have of course no information that would help us decide whether such fetish formation appearing at the ages of four and five indicates some widespread pathology or foreshadows later perverse development. It may be that such fetishes in the phallic phase appear much more commonly than we have heretofore suspected. Such quantitative factors as the intensity of the castration anxiety and the degree of disturbance in the preoedipal years may ultimately be crucial for the differentiation of those cases in which the fetish goes on to become an obligate prop for sexual functioning in adulthood from those in which this childhood manifestation finds a more normal resolution.

Of the cases described by Wulff, perhaps the most evocative as far as its bearing on the subject of the infantile fetish is concerned is the little boy whose transitional object of the first year, his mother's nightgown, shifted in the second year to a brassiere or stockings which she had worn. When this case was described to Freud, the latter wrote: "It has been shown beyond doubt... that the fetish is a penis substitute, a substitute for the missing penis of the mother, and hence a means of defense against castration anxiety — and nothing else. There remains to test this in the case of this child. If proof is to be forthcoming the boy must have had ample opportunity to convince himself of his naked mother's lack of a penis" (quoted by Wulff, p. 462). Freud's expectations were completely fulfilled. The parents, whose bedroom the boy shared, undressed in his presence, in order, as the mother put it, to accustom him to their naked bodies and to enable him to recognize the difference between the sexes. Freud, then, would seem to have accepted this use of stocking and brassiere in a 16-month-old boy as definite evidence of a fetishistic defense against castration anxiety.

Wulff raised an understandable objection to Freud's formulation in this case, an objection that cannot be wished away. He states that such a possibility "is in complete contradiction to our very certain and well-established knowledge concerning the development of the child and its various phases." He (p. 464) quotes Freud (1923b, p. 144): "It seems to me, however, that *the significance of the castration complex can only be rightly appreciated if its origin in the phase of phallic primacy is also taken into account.*"

Greenacre (1970), aware of this conceptual dilemma, offered the following solution:

> It is my impression that early fetish formation does not develop unless the accompanying disturbances have been so undermining as to produce a severe preoedipal castration problem, whether through illness, operative procedure, or severe parental mishandling. It is significant that at the early age of one to two years there is a general body responsiveness to discomfort or physical insult, and discharge of tension may occur through whatever channels are available at this special time. If the disturbance is so severe, however, that ordinary discharge mechanisms are inadequate, premature genital stimulation may be induced. This is most likely to occur during the second year. This tends

then to promote sadomasochistic elements in the incipient erotic response. Some fluidity between pregenital and genital responses remains, and gives rise to a tendency to persistent polymorphous perverse reactions as well as increasing later castration problems [pp. 336–337].

In brief, then, Greenacre states that under the special conditions of a highly disturbed preoedipal development, premature genital stimulation may be induced during the second year, and produces severe preoedipal castration problems. Strong sadomasochistic tendencies appear coupled with the emergence of an infantile fetish resembling in many respects that of the adult fetish, of which it is sometimes the antecedent.

The construct of the infantile fetish as a true genetic forerunner of that in the adult perversion would then require that we can demonstrate the existence of a fetish that has the same general dynamic outline as the adult fetish and that appears with some regularity earlier than the phallic-oedipal phase, that is, during the second year of life. It would be necessary to demonstrate that the infant's profound attachment to the fetish object follows the development of an intense preoedipal castration reaction and that the fetish is a defense expressed in concrete form to both stabilize the primary genital outline of the body image and support the delusion of a maternal phallus. The need for the fetish emerges out of seriously compromised early object relatedness and body-image formation. It is a reflection of significant disruption in the cohesiveness of the developing ego organization and certainly contributes to a variety of later disturbances, whether adult perversions or serious character deformations.

Anna Freud (1965), in her discussion of the fetish of childhood and its relation to the adult perversion, correctly cautions us: "Seen from the side of the analyses of relevant adult cases, there is no doubt of the early origin of their fetish and of its persistent nature. . . Seen from the side of clinical experience with children, on the other hand, it is equally obvious that the number of childhood fetishes is far greater than that of the true fetishists of later years" (p. 211).

Unfortunately, the literature is replete with many confusing references to an infantile fetish when the clinical observations or the theoretical arguments clearly suggest that what is being considered is a transitional object, with emphasis on the ubiquitous and healthy aspect of the phenomenon. We agree with Winnicott (1953), in his discussion of Wulff's paper, when he states: "There is a difference between my point of view and that of Wulff which is reflected in my use of this special term [transitional object] and his use of the term 'fetish object.' A study of Wulff's paper seems to show that in using the word fetish he has taken back to infancy something that belongs in ordinary theory to the sexual perversions. . . I would prefer to retain the word fetish to describe the object that is employed on account of a *delusion* of a maternal phallus" (p. 96).

We would like to offer a developmental outline for the emergence of a true infantile fetish in the preoedipal stage. In our clinical observations we have found a ubiquitous early genital-zone arousal appearing regularly between 15 and 24 months of age, reflected in a significantly increased frequency and intensity of genital manipulation including organized masturbatory activity. This early sexual arousal seems normally to be involved with the consolidation of the object and body-self representations and particularly with the establishment of the primary genital outline of the body image, which plays a nuclear role in establishing a sense of sexual identity.

In our study population, which we have reason to believe represents a fairly random selection of families, all the infants, in the context of this upsurge in sexual curiosity, have had the experience of perceiving the anatomical difference between the sexes. The four boys and at least six of the girls who subsequently developed severe castration reactions during the second year, formed an intense and persistent attachment to a fetish object, frequently displacing an earlier attachment to a transitional object. The fetish object served partially to bind the sharp and highly disruptive upsurge in hostile aggression consequent to the severe castration reaction and partially to stabilize uncertain object and body-self representations, particularly the primary genital outline of the body image.

The earlier history of these infants who developed severe castration reactions with a consequent attachment to a fetish object indicated that all were subject to intense strain during the first year of life. Although these infants differentiate psychologically in the latter half of the first year, they do so under much greater than ordinary strain. They are subject to much more intense anxiety over object loss and body-self dissolution than is usual. Their severe castration reactions are accompanied by a sharp increment in the level of both anxiety and object-directed aggression. These sequelae, particularly the intensification of hostile aggression, further undermine the already uncertain self and object representations and seriously interfere with ego development, particularly the integrative function of the ego. Instead of developing an enhanced independence supported by a relatively secure mental representation of the maternal object, which normally is partially consolidated by the end of the second year, these infants show an intense hostile dependence on the mother with a tendency to shadow her, thus constricting their developing autonomy.

We believe that these are the developmental conditions for the emergence of a predominantly negative oedipal configuration in both boys and girls during the later phallic phase. Since the development of object constancy is seriously compromised by the increment of hostile aggression, these youngsters react to the ordinary castration insults characteristic of the phallic-oedipal phase with intense castration anxiety which is amplified by both object loss and body-self dissolution anxiety.

Clinical Observations

Let us return to some of the infants whose development we have already described. Suzy (see Chapter 7) will be recalled as manifesting a moderate castration reaction at 17 to 19 months.

For the purpose of our discussion of the infantile fetish, the story begins at Christmastime when Suzy, aged 16½ months, was given, among other gifts, a battery-operated, walking-talking doll almost as large as she was. Suzy was at first somewhat taken aback by this rather formidable toy, but when a flap in the doll's back became unhinged and the batteries fell out, she broke out into intense, frightened crying. The doll was quickly repaired, but Suzy would have nothing further to do with it, and it was put away in a closet in her room. Some six weeks later the family moved to a new, larger apartment. While Suzy did not show any particular anxiety in connection with this move, she asked to have this doll in her crib and fell asleep clinging to the doll and a soft woolen coverlet to which she had previously had no special attachment. The new attachment to the doll and coverlet continued unabated for the remaining three months that we observed Suzy. She would fall asleep pressing the coverlet with one hand against her cheek and sucking her thumb, and holding her other arm around her doll. Whenever any other children visited, she very generously permitted them to use any one of her toys — with the exception of this now very precious doll. She could not tolerate having any child touch this doll.

Ruth (see Chapter 6), whose congenital defect required that she wear a corrective pillow between her diaper and her perineal area from the ages of three months to one year, developed an intense attachment to a doll she called "boy" at the height of her castration reaction. Her favorite inanimate companions were a number of dolls which she carried with her everywhere without using them in play.

Ruth's use of dolls at this critical time suggests that they now served in part as infantile fetishistic objects in an effort to repair her sense of the defective genital. We have come to realize that the doll has a complicated series of meanings, some deriving from early stages of development, when they have a "transitional object" quality, while others serve a much more advanced state of symbolization. We have noted regression in semisymbolic play with dolls, just as in other areas of symbolization, and consider this to be important evidence of disturbed development.

Billy (see Chapter 4), whose early development was strained consequent to his mother's severe anxiety and his father's absence from the time he was nine months old through his second year, at 15 months of age developed a sharp but unusually circumscribed castration reaction. In this context a new obligatory going-to-sleep ritual emerged in which he fell asleep lying prone with his baby bottle pressed against his penis. The choice of the bottle as a fetishistic defense against castration concerns probably reflects Billy's fear of object loss.

Billy's direct manual masturbation began to recede as he masturbated by lying prone with some inanimate object (the bottle, a toy, or ball) pressed against his penis. That the masturbatory pattern took on the form of the going-to-sleep ritual signaled a major intrusion into the early genital sexual current of significant defensive elements against concerns about object loss and body dissolution. The intrusion of these defensive elements into the masturbatory pattern probably accounts for the increasing prominence of Billy's masturbatory activity. The significant expression of defense by an action, i.e., in the masturbatory activity, probably also accounts for the very limited psychological elaboration of defense against castration concerns noted in Billy.

We are grateful to Dr. Daniel Feinberg for permitting us to read and discuss with him his unpublished manuscript, "An Analysis of Intractable Nightmares in a Two-Year-Old Boy." The case material affords us a vivid and interesting example of an infantile fetish in the process of formation. A 26-month-old boy developed a profound sleep disturbance as a consequence of repetitive nightmares, so that he averaged only two to three hours of sleep at night. During the long periods of wakefulness, he was overactive but not in a prolonged panic. His parents had divorced when he was a little over 12 months of age, and for roughly four months after the separation he suffered a mild sleep disturbance. His nighttime awakenings were frequent but not persistent or prolonged, and unaccompanied by nightmares as best one could determine. At that time his mother's reassurance enabled him to return easily to sleep.

At the onset of the severe sleep disturbance which led him to treatment he threw out of his crib all the stuffed animals with which he had previously been accustomed to fall asleep, calling them "No good." In their place, he insisted on taking to bed with him each night his toy trucks and cars.

We could clearly establish that this little boy had for several months shown a real interest in his penis and had engaged in genital masturbation. It was also established that he had recently had the opportunity to see his mother's and a little girl cousin's genitals exposed. The precise details and timing could not be ascertained, except that it had all taken place before the boy fell ill. The therapeutic work with this boy disclosed the nuclear role of the castration complex in the entire symptomatic picture; it also provided clear evidence that the infantile fetishes, the toy trucks and cars, stood for the penis, the absent father, and the missing penis of the mother.

In each of the cases presented, we have been able to offer reasonably convincing evidence of a primary sexual arousal. That is to say, with the increase in spontaneous, endogenous genital sensation, the infant's attention is increasingly drawn to the genitals, which as a consequence gradually attain a greater and more distinct narcissistic importance for the infant than does, for example, the toe or the elbow. We have already suggested that with the delay in the immediate discharge of bowel and bladder tension that takes place in the early part of the second year, independent of any parental efforts to establish toilet control, there regularly and normally occurs a spread in excitation to and arousal of the genital organs. Greenacre (1968) presented a strikingly parallel formulation when she wrote, "I have thought that toward the end of the second year there was regularly some enhancement of genital sensitivity (phallic or clitoral) that occurred simultaneously with the increasing maturation of the body sphincters" (p. 304).

In a later paper, however, Greenacre (1970) offered what seems to be a contradictory formulation when she stated that under the special conditions of a highly disturbed preoedipal development, there may be a premature genitalization and a severe preoedipal castration complex.

The transitional object is a support in the period at the inception of autonomous ego development and object relatedness, and furthers the union of the (nonhostile) aggression of growth with loving tenderness...It would appear, however, that when the infant has suffered unusually severe deprivation or mistreatment, i.e., when the mother has not been good enough to neutralize this, the hostile elements in the aggression appear in mounting tension from frustration, and the energy cannot be sufficiently used in the forward movement of growth. It then finds discharge in rages, or it may become bodybound, gradually causing premature sadomasochistic erotization associated sometimes with precocious genitalization under strain [p. 336].

In this passage, Greenacre is describing the infants who develop severe castration reactions in the second year of life. We have already described the sharp upsurge in hostile aggression these infants direct at the mother. We assume that when Greenacre says that this aggression finds discharge in rages or becomes bodybound, leading to sadomasochistic erotization, she means that the purely destructive aim of the aggression is blunted through its fusion with a libidinal current, leading to a sadomasochistic object relationship. With this erotization of the aggression, Greenacre suggests, there may be a premature genital-zone arousal.

While we have certainly seen evidences of such development—for example, in Billy's clutching his penis through his diapers whenever he was frustrated or enraged—we would tend to view this behavior as a special and pathological variant of the normal sexual arousal that regularly occurs during this period of life.

We believe that castration reactions frequently appear at this period precisely because the genitals normally attain a particular and heightened narcissistic valence as a consequence of the regular genital arousal. We do not think that a castration reaction appearing at this time is of necessity a major pathological complex which bespeaks an ominous disruption in development. We believe that the intensity of the castration reaction and its consequent effect on subsequent development vary as a function of the severity of the insults the infant has experienced in the object and body spheres, whether through maternal mishandling, birth defect, illness, or operative procedures.

Normally, the sexual arousal which is characteristic of the second year concerns itself with the expansion and consolidation of the self and object representations. The three research infants just described already had an uncertain sense of self and object, and their discovery of the anatomical difference between the sexes and the emergence of severe castration reactions led to an intensification of hostile aggression. This served to disrupt and seriously interfere with the whole individuation thrust as well as with some of the major aspects of ego development such as play, symbolization, defense, and frustration tolerance.

In the two little girls whose fetishistic attachments we have described in this chapter, the awareness of the genital difference produced the additional burden of disappointment and anger, which very much intensified the hostile aspect of the ambivalence that is characteristic of this stage of development. In all these infants, the intensification of the hostility resulted in the mobilization of the defense mechanism of the splitting of the maternal image with the projection of the bad object (Mahler, 1971). This was reflected in each toddler by the explosive expansion of the fear of object loss and a recrudescence of the fear of strangers. All these infants developed a heightened dependence on their mothers, almost literally clinging to them, and demonstrated a sullen mistrust of other adults and children, which did not portend well for the age-appropriate push toward individuation.

Simultaneously, a split in the self representation seemed to have occurred, with the obligatory infantile fetish serving to bolster the genital outline of the body. In the two girls described in this chapter, the walking-talking doll and the doll "boy" served to deny the absence of their own penis. In the little boy, the bedtime ritual with the bottle served not only to deny the absent penis of the mother but also to bolster the genital outline of his own body in the face of the confusion which must arise from the two competing genital schemata, the tactile, visual, and sensorimotor schema of his own body and the schema that arises through a primary identification with the visual percept of his mother's genitals.

The intense hostile aggression in these infants arises as a result of the early disturbance in the mother-child relationship as well as the castration reaction. The increased ambivalence in these infants not only has the effect of weakening the developing self and object representations, but also seems to call forth a turning of aggression against the self, a mechanism which was particularly notable in Ruth, but also quite prominent in Suzy. Finally, the heightened aggression would seem to

foster an early erotization of aggression, as was indicated, for example, by Billy's tendency to masturbate
when frustrated or angered and the distinct development of teasing in Suzy and Ruth.

To sum up, then, in the infants we have described,
the appearance of the infantile fetish in the second year
of life was preceded by definite indications of a sexual
arousal, the observation of the anatomical difference
between the sexes, and a distinct and prominent castration reaction. We are therefore suggesting the existence
of a true infantile fetish, that is, a fetish having a clear
dynamic continuity with the fetish arising later in life.
The fetish serves to define and supplement the representation of the body, particularly the genital outline of the
body. This reparative construct is precipitated and split
off as a result of the undermining of the sense of body integrity that follows from the observation of the anatomical difference between the sexes at a time in life when
the genitals have already assumed a distinct narcissistic
importance.

The infantile fetish arises in the setting of an already compromised earlier development and resembles
in many respects the adult fetish, of which it may be an
antecedent. The fetish is a defense expressed in concrete
form. It emerges out of early inadequate object relations
and is part of defective ego and drive development, all
of which undoubtedly contribute to a variety of types of
later psychopathology. It may even be that the infantile
fetish and fetishistic phenomena are much more common than we have tended to think, but that perhaps in
all but the most severe castration reactions of early life,
the young child's reliance on the fetish as a supplement

to the body concept is ultimately diffused through its extension into play, fantasy, character formation, and other less tangible and concrete defensive forms.

CHAPTER 11

A DELAYED
EARLY GENITAL AROUSAL

A significant number of infants develop at some time in the first year of life a profound, protracted, painful true constipation. A very small number of these infants have manifest structural defects, such as Hirschsprung's Disease where there is a constitutional narrowing of the rectal and anal passage. By far the largest number of constipated infants, however, have no structural problem, and pediatric gastroenterologists vaguely explain their symptoms as a functional immaturity of the large intestines. We have been fortunate in being able to follow in considerable detail the development through their second year of several children who had suffered this latter type of severe functional constipation. One particularly well-studied case has led us to think that these severe constipations developing in the first year may be variants of the normal differentiation process.

SALLY

Sally was adopted at the age of two weeks and was an entirely normal, sturdy, vigorous newborn. Her parents had been married for six years and had been actively but unsuccessfully trying to have a baby for four years before they adopted her. Two weeks after Sally was adopted, her mother found she was pregnant, but almost at the same time began spotting. Her gynecologist told her that there might be some reason for spotting, such as fetal abnormality, and since she already had the responsibility of caring for the four-week-old Sally, he advised that she not confine herself to bed. Several times over the next three months when the bleeding became heavier, she was convinced that she had miscarried. When Sally was four months old her mother was admitted to the hospital with severe cramping and heavy bleeding, and within a few days miscarried. Sally was left for the period of hospitalization in the care of her mother's older sister. On her mother's return Sally did not smile at her for a week and, for the first two days, did not even seem to recognize her. Her mother was convinced that Sally hated her.

When Sally was eight months old and showing distinct behavioral indications of a sharp differentiation thrust, she suddenly exploded with object-directed aggression. Daily, frequently in situations of quite minor frustration but most often where no context could be established, the infant would suddenly and fiercely bite her mother's hand or body. These bites hurt and often badly so; Sally's mother was always startled and frequently enraged by the suddenness and fierceness of the biting attacks. When angered, she would take Sally's hand and firmly place it in Sally's mouth with the implied communication, "Don't bite me, bite yourself!" Quite remarkably, within three weeks, the biting attacks on the mother all but stopped. Now, whenever the infant was angry, which was not infrequent, instead of biting her mother, Sally would sharply bite her own hand or on occasion bite the side of her crib or some other inanimate object. Over the next week or two the biting stopped completely. Instead, Sally, when she was clearly angry, would pull her own hair. After some six weeks the overt expression of object-directed aggression distinctly and rapidly diminished, and by age 10 months it had virtually disappeared. Over the next year when actively disturbed or intensely frustrated, some resurgence of hair-pulling and biting of the self and mother occurred, but these were relatively brief and self-limited periods of a week or two and rapidly subsided and disappeared.

Within a week after the emergence of the object-directed aggression Sally, at eight months, developed a profound and persistent painful constipation characterized by as many as four or five bouts of cramping each day, lasting for periods of a few minutes to as long as a half hour. During these bouts her body became pronouncedly rigid, her face flushed, and she screamed loudly as she strained at her stool. The constipation continued unremittingly until Sally was 10 months old when she just as abruptly developed a persistent non-infectious diarrhea which lasted for eight weeks. Shortly before her first birthday the constipation reappeared with all its former severity and continued unremittingly for over five months.

When Sally was 17 months old her parents took a one-week vacation, leaving her with her maternal aunt. On their return she developed a moderately severe separation reaction with a sleep disturbance that lasted some two weeks, an otitis (Heinicke and Westheimer, 1965), and a pronounced intensification of the constipation. The mother now bought a potty which Sally eagerly used. Within several weeks, with very little urging or support from the mother, Sally developed reliable bowel control, night and day, and within several weeks was trained for urine as well. A remarkable sequel to the toilet training was the rapid easing of the constipation, so that by 19 months the straining virtually disappeared. Sally's bowel function remained more or less normal over the next year that we continued to follow her.

Coincident with the toilet training and the easing of the constipation was a remarkable expansion and surge in Sally's general development. The babyish and masklike countenance rapidly gave way to a highly mobile face which reflected a wide range of expression. Her affective range until this time had been bland and narrow. Now her activity was vigorous, exuberant, and highly social. Her language expanded remarkably and her symbolic fantasy and play became quite sophisticated.

Some features of Sally's sexual development were also of interest. Early in the second year, she had been observed on a number of occasions to touch her genitals, laugh, and hold her finger up to her mother. There were, however, no indications of an organized masturbatory pattern. It was only after the toilet training had gained some pace and the constipation disappeared that some clear indications of a moderate castration reaction emerged. For example, she would point to her father's nipples and call them "penis." She was observed to handle and pull at the penis of the anatomically accurate doll and then feed the nipple of another doll (not the anatomic variety) with a bottle full of water, after which, sitting on the pot and urinating, she mouthed the doll's hair. The word vagina completely dropped out of her vocabulary. Direct genital touching with her hand also stopped, but she was observed to rub her genitals vigorously and for long periods of time with large wads of toilet paper after she urinated.

Sally's mother was intelligent and devoted, though extremely reserved, not only with the research staff but also with the other mothers. Because she was not very forthcoming in talking about her personal feelings, we knew little about how she felt at not being able to bear a child of her own and about the adoption — which is not to suggest that we had any question about her love for Sally. We have, however, wondered whether Sally's unusually early sense of her separateness may not have had something to do with her having been adopted — the mother, not having carried Sally, lacked the psychophysiological preparedness for symbiosis. This mother rarely showed an ability to lose her boundaries and to merge easily with her daughter. The one question she ever posed about child rearing was when to tell Sally of her adoption. On being asked whether she herself was ever constipated, she replied that that would have nothing to do with Sally's constipation, since she was adopted. To the question, "Who does the child take after?", we received the same reply. One day in the nursery when Sally was 17½ months old, in the midst of a moderately intense separation reaction, she sat on the potty straining at her stool off and on for half an hour, feet rigidly extended, face beet-red, and screaming with pain. The harrowed staff observer said to Sally's mother, "It must be hard for you." She replied, not without compassion, "Sally is the one who is suffering. It's hard on her."

Whatever role the foregoing may play, we are strongly convinced that the mother's unexpected pregnancy when Sally was four weeks old had a major impact on her relationship to the infant. The serious conflict between the demand for the active nurturing care of Sally and the requirement of absolute bed-rest in the face of the sustained vaginal spotting for the integrity of the fetus she carried was understandably an insoluble one and made serious inroads into her emotional availability to Sally. Sally's reaction to the separation of three days when the mother had the miscarriage would not be at all unusual in a child during the latter half of the first year or during the second year and would hardly warrant much attention. Such an organized reaction to separation in an infant of four months, however, suggesting as it does some significant level in the sense of separateness and in the operation of object-directed aggression, does command consideration. We assume that the mother's conflict over her pregnancy and her consequent relative emotional unavailability to Sally forced a precocious sense of separateness, the emergence of object-directed aggression, as well as some instability in Sally's developing sense of self and object. This assumption would account for the sharp and sustained object-directed aggression Sally manifested at eight months in the midst of a vigorous differentiation push. Normally at this point in development, such aggression remains potential rather than actual, supported by a ready, easy tendency toward a transitory dedifferentiation whenever aggression tends to be mobilized. That is, the infant's ready capacity for regression to a symbiotic unity with the mother in the face of the daily ubiquitous points of strain, such as frustration and the actual or emotional unavailability of the mother, serves to blunt the aggression since it blurs the sharp sense of separateness.

In Sally, this normal moratorium in the actualization of aggression did not hold. We assume that the precociously developed sense of separateness, the fragility of the representations of self and object did not support the normal, easy dedifferentiation; that is, the very uncertainty and instability of these schema resulted in a defensive rigidity in their structure which resisted an easy regression.

The vicissitudes of the object-directed aggression resulted in a developmental variant of considerable interest. The immediate and most obvious course was the turning of the aggression against the self, reflected in Sally's biting her own hand and later pulling her own hair whenever she was angry at her mother. The hair-pulling demonstrates very dramatically the aggressivization of the hand; that is, the scratching, grasping hand takes on the oral-aggressive mode (Hoffer, 1949).

The aggressivization of the hand is not at all uncommon in early developmental deviations where the infant has to deal with a considerable amount of object-directed aggression at a time when the rudimentary structures of self and object are still unstable. This mechanism is implicated in the early history of a number of developing perversions where direct manual masturbation seems not to develop since the hand function is too aggressivized. Instead, the masturbation involves the nonmanual rubbing of the genitals against either transitional objects, an infantile fetish, or other inanimate objects.

Sally's turning of her aggression against herself was undoubtedly supported by her mother's angry intolerance of it. When the mother angrily placed Sally's hand in Sally's mouth, in addition to the implied message, "Don't bite me, bite yourself," was the message, "When you bite me, I get so angry I would like to bite you back."

However, this mother's individual response to her infant's aggression aside, it does seem to us that there is a developmental necessity to blunt the aggression in order to preserve the integrity of the still unstable self and object representations and the coherence of the nascent ego organization.

When, as in Sally's case, an unusually sharp differentiation thrust occurs in the context of an intense primary ambivalence, the developmental variant of a precocious anal-zone arousal seems to serve to channel object-directed aggression while still preserving the basic attachment to the external object world and insuring the coherence of the developing ego organization. This relatively benign variant is in sharp contrast to other developmental variants in which object relatedness and ego development are more compromised and deviant, as exemplified in the symbiotic psychoses (see Chapter 2), where the intense aggression mobilized consequent to the differentiation process threatens the cohesiveness of the ego and the basic structure of self and object representations. The object-loss and self-dissolution panic evoked in these cases results in a sharp regression to a symbiotic self-object relatedness and a massive compromise of ego development.

The anal channeling of the aggression and its binding in the constipation was perhaps most vividly demonstrated when Sally was 17 months old, following her parents' return from a week-long holiday. Unlike most children of this age, whose separation reaction will include a significant outbreak of overt aggression directed at the mother, Sally, while showing no direct aggression, developed a remarkable intensification of the chronic constipation.

We speculate that the investment of the anal zone and its stool product with libido as well as hostile aggression is the normal drive distribution characteristic of the anal phase. The tension between the two drive cathexes probably accounts for the new level of bowel withholding, straining, and the shift in attention to the bowel movement that are usual at this stage. The libido with its oral introjective mode tends to incorporate the stool-object, whereas the tendency of the hostile aggression is to shatter and destroy the stool-object. We assume that the investment of the stool-object with both sexual and aggressive drives accounts for the normal erotization of aggression which is ubiquitously observable in the emergence of some level of sadistic teasing during this stage.

The anal-zone arousal and the apparent investment of the stool-object with sexual and aggressive drive
cathexis would seem to establish some transitional,
intermediate area of object relatedness in which the
stool product stands for the object and yet is not the object, stands for the self and yet is not the self, in much
the same manner as Winnicott's (1953) transitional object and phenomena (cf. Furer, 1964). This has the
adaptive advantage of blurring the sharp sense of separateness while permitting further consolidation of the
self and object representations. While there continues to
be something of the same level of concreteness of the
symbol, stool-object, as was the case with Winnicott's
earlier transitional-stage blanket-object, there is now a
considerable advance in that the process is significantly
internalized.

There is a continuum of developmental contexts
deviant from the optimal in which drive cathexes are
distributed in alternative, variable ways. In the extreme
we have childhood autism in which there is no significant investment in an object external to the self and,
consequently, at this stage no investment of the anal
zone and its stool product. We are proposing on the
basis of the few cases we have observed the far less deviant variant characterized by the constipations, relatively fixed or more transient, or the noninfectious diarrheas which are frequently observable after some level
of differentiation out of the symbiotic phase has been attained. The constipations seem to develop in situations
in which there is a relative increment in hostile aggression consequent to object-loss concerns greater than

usual at this stage. In these cases the increment in aggression seems to mobilize a compensatory increment in the libidinal cathexis of the stool. The diarrheas seem to result from the rapid increments in hostile aggression where there is no complementary shift in libidinal cathexis.

Toilet training, which is usual during the second or third year, normally involves some resolution of the phase-specific separation conflicts in that the child actively holds onto or releases the stool-object. It is our impression that with toilet control, and, perhaps more centrally, with the partial resolution of the phase-specific separation conflicts, ego structures gradually are precipitated that have the capacity to modify and modulate the aggressive drive so that the impact is not as intense or its aim so totally destructive. This seems to be the developmental precondition for the integration of the bad hated object and the good loved object which is characteristic of object constancy (Mahler et al., 1975, p. 110).

In this connection it was indeed remarkable that when Sally established firm toilet control at 19 months, the heretofore chronic constipation rapidly disappeared. The extraordinary expansion and surge in her development following the establishment of toilet control, the variegated and subtle register of mood and expression, reflecting as it does a new level of affective modulation, all suggest a significant expansion of the differentiation process. It seems to us that this expansion follows from some resolution of the transitional function of the anal-zone arousal and the stool product, which up to this point served to blur the sharp sense of separateness; that is, the more rigidly defensive transitional function of the stool-object in these constipations, although initially adaptive, resists the expansion of the individuation thrust.

We assume that Sally, despite her mother's relative emotional unavailability, was given a sufficiently positive nurturing core to permit a precocious anal-zone arousal and an ambivalent cathexis of the stool product, which resulted in the constipation. This maneuver has the adaptive advantage of binding the aggression while preserving a tie to the object world, the coherence of the ego, and the relative integrity of the whole developmental thrust.

Basic to our conceptualization of the structure of the constipation is the mobilization of the differentiation process under conditions of more than ordinary strain, the precocious emergence of drive differentiation, and the ambivalent cathexis of the stool product.

We find intriguing one final detail in Sally's development. She showed only a shadowy early genital-zone arousal, which was in sharp contrast to the general vigor of her development. Only after the resolution of the constipation did Sally manifest an organized masturbation pattern and a castration reaction of some dimension. It seems to us that this significant delay in the emergence of the early genital phase was a consequence of the extensive ambivalent drive cathexis of the anal zone and the stool product, with the latter taking on a self-object meaning. Whatever the dynamics of the resultant blurring of the sense of separateness, this phenomenon seems invariably to delay the emergence of the early genital-zone arousal.

CHAPTER 12

A DISTURBANCE IN
SEXUAL IDENTITY

Malcolm was one of the boys preselected as having experienced a sufficiently traumatic first year so that he would be expected to develop a severe castration reaction. Unfortunately, this expectation was fulfilled, and his subsequent course demonstrated many aspects of confused sexual identity during the latter part of his second year and his third year as well.

Although we will not attempt to review the extensive literature concerning the etiology of the perversions, Greenacre's (1953a, 1955, 1960, 1970) and Bak's (1968) contributions are particularly relevant for their reference to preoedipal factors. Greenacre's contributions have already been reviewed (see Chapter 9). Bak, although he insisted upon the central role of the castration complex during the phallic phase in the subsequent development of the perversions, nonetheless agreed that there are forerunners of the bisexual identification. These forerunners consist of early patterns of primary identification and disturbances in the separation-individuation phase.

Bak also noted that patients with sadomasochistic perversions, according to their history, appear to have had a very intense relationship with the mother in early infancy, with much physical closeness to her, and that they are extremely vulnerable and sensitive to separation. Bak believed that the intense rage these patients experienced in reaction to separation resulted in the erotization of aggression. Phallic activity became so imbued with aggression that it could not be discharged in the sexual act lest the partner be destroyed.

The little boy described in this chapter showed certain early developmental patterns that were strikingly similar to those described by both Bak and Greenacre. His case gives us an opportunity to correlate reconstructive formulations with direct observation. Malcolm's mother was a severely depressed and anxious woman whose intense and hostile ambivalence toward her son seriously interfered with his attempts at differentiation and separation. Malcolm's prolonged symbiotic attachment was additionally fortified by an unduly close body intimacy with both parents. A number of experiences at the beginning of his second year added to his vulnerability and culminated in a severe crisis during the period of genital discovery at 18 months of age. We describe the confusion in sexual identity and the peculiar fetishistic use of inanimate objects that emerged as he attempted to deal with his severe castration anxiety and his fears of object loss and self-annihilation.

MALCOLM

According to the history obtained when Malcolm, an only child of 15 months of age, entered our research nursery, his parents considered that his development had been uneventful and entirely within average limits. There were, however, features we considered to be distinctly unusual. Breast-feeding had been abruptly discontinued when he was five days old because the parents were planning a short outing with Malcolm that they felt would interfere with the nursing process. This ambivalent pattern of behavior, consisting of initial closeness often followed by sudden withdrawal, characterized the relations between this child and his parents during his first year and thereafter. Mother and infant were rarely apart. The mother maintained few contacts outside of the home and pursued no interests of her own. The parents rarely went out in the evenings, and on the few occasions when they did, Malcolm was already asleep. Whenever Malcolm cried, he was immediately soothed by back-rubbing and rocking, so that he was given no opportunity to learn how to tolerate delay or frustration. Furthermore, intimacy with his parents was extended to being bathed with them very frequently from his sixth month on, as well as constantly witnessing their toileting activities.

The intense family intimacy was abruptly interrupted for the first time when Malcolm was eight months old. He was left with his grandparents for 10 days at their home, which he had never visited before. About a week after his parents returned, Malcolm began to refuse food when his mother tried to feed him.

Just after Malcolm's first birthday, his mother became pregnant, and one month later the family moved to another city. Within a week of the move, Malcolm suddenly developed an intense fear of the vacuum cleaner, and shortly thereafter lacerated his lip severely when he fell in the bathtub. This accident resulted in profuse bleeding, a frantic trip to the hospital, and mummying and suturing without anesthesia. These incidents were followed by several weeks of severe family upheaval during which Malcolm was inconsolable. His mother rocked, patted, and rubbed him almost constantly, and took several long baths with him each day in order to comfort him. Furthermore, his father's presence now frightened him for the first time, and he cried whenever his father approached.

In addition to his general distress, his oral behavior showed a distinct change. Malcolm had used both his bottle and his thumb for sucking before the accident; now he completely renounced both and never again returned to his bottle. At the same time he became attached to a large stuffed bear, which the family called Boo, and to a favorite blanket. Although both of these objects had been in his crib all along, they had never before been of special interest to him. After his accident, he insisted upon having his blanket with him constantly, and he spent many hours cuddling and hugging his stuffed bear. It was noted, however, that he bit off the bear's nose during one of the cuddling sessions, and his intense anger frequently culminated in temper tantrums.

A marked increase in genital handling completed the array of Malcolm's reactions to his lip accident and the other events of his life. Malcolm had begun to reach for his own and his father's penis during his fifth or sixth month, a precocious emergence of genital awareness, and intermittent genital touching had been present from that time onward. Following the accident there was a distinct change in this genital behavior. He tried to pull off his diaper repeatedly in order to get at and hold his penis, and he grasped at his penis very frequently whenever his diaper was removed, behavior most unusual in an infant of this age.

As already mentioned, the early relationship between mother and child had been an intensely symbiotic one, with the additional intimacy of repeated tactile and kinesthetic nude body contact during his bathing with both parents. Visual exposure during both bathing and toileting had also been extensive. We have also described the unusually ambivalent quality of the mother-child relationship reflected in the sudden weaning at five days, the mother's inability to frustrate Malcolm or be separated from him, the sudden abandonment to his unfamiliar grandparents at eight months, and the overanxious solicitude with which his mother treated him at all times, but particularly after his lip injury at 13 months of age.

Against the background of his unusual general development and the special quality of his relationship with his mother, we would like to consider the nature of Malcolm's genital play, reported to have begun at five or six months and to have continued after that without interruption. In the literature concerning the onset and vicissitudes of genital arousal during the first year of life, genital play is considered an aspect of general body exploration as well as a reflection of the mother-child relationship. Loewenstein (1950) and Casuso (1957) both reported normally developing infant boys who discovered their penis at 10 months of age. The boy Kleeman (1965) described was eight months old when genital handling first occurred, but this was not repeated until he was 10 months. Spitz and Wolf (1949) found that the development of genital play depends upon the quality of the relationship between mother and child, and that genital play did not appear at all in infants reared in institutions where there was no contact with the mother. Although there is general agreement that the erotic component in this early genital handling is secondary, if present at all, Kleeman (1965) suggests that the child is simulating his whole experience with his mother, including those genital erotic sensations which have been aroused by her.

Data concerning early genital discovery in our research sample indicate that the average age of discovery in these boys was somewhere between eight and 10 months, and their genital exploration continued to be brief, episodic, and very casual until the later period of genital interest at 15 or 16 months of age. Four of the boys in our group discovered their genitals at four or five months, and their genital play was more frequent, of greater intensity, and more protracted than the others.

Malcolm was one of this group of boys with early genital discovery, all of whom had the experience of considerable exposure to body intimacy with at least one and frequently both parents during their first eight or 10 months of life. Such extensive tactile, kinesthetic, and visual stimulation is apparently conducive to the emergence of premature genital arousal, the possible consequences of which we shall discuss subsequently.

Another important aspect of Malcolm's first year was the oral zone disturbance which was reflected in his persistent refusal to let his mother feed him after the sudden separation at eight months. The abrupt abandonment, with the transition from the intense intimacy of the close family unit to the strangeness of his grandparents and their unfamiliar home, apparently stimulated anger of such intensity that it seriously interfered with the mother-child relationship. Furthermore, the series of events that began just after Malcolm's first birthday came at a particularly vulnerable period in general, with the onset of independent locomotion and the period of autonomy. The family move, the beginning of the mother's pregnancy, and his lip injury with its attendant pain, physical restraint, and interference with sucking, affected Malcolm to a very marked degree. His increased separation anxiety and heightened hostile aggression were clearly evident as he clung to his mother, feared his father for the first time, and exploded into tantrums. The infant's growing attachment to the father at the end of the first year aids in separating from the mother, as we have said earlier, and in the infant's emergence from his symbiotic attachment to the mother. However, excessive anger toward the mother may endanger the very existence of this relationship, so that some of the anger may then be split off and projected onto another object. If the father is available, he himself may become the recipient of the anger, as in this case.

Oral gratification was no longer available (Malcolm had given up thumb and bottle after his lip accident) and hostile aggression to the mother had increased. It is likely that Malcolm shifted his attachment abruptly and massively to his first transitional objects — a bear and a blanket — for these reasons. The usual function of such objects is to blur the sense of separateness to fulfill libidinal needs, and to help maintain a sense of body integrity. Malcolm's need for these objects was highly exaggerated because the various traumatic experiences to which he had been subjected had made it far more difficult for him to develop a sense of the physical integrity of his own body, as well as a reliable sense of the object as a separate entity.

The markedly intensified genital handling during this period was probably due to Malcolm's intense rage, which could not be adequately discharged through the ordinary channels. Instead, the genital pathway, which had been activated precociously at five or six months in connection with the intense body intimacy between child and parents, was now utilized for the discharge of aggression as well.

Such was the background of this mother and infant when they entered our nursery in the early part of Malcolm's 15th month. Malcolm needed to maintain constant physical contact with his mother in the nursery, a situation that holds some threat of both stranger and separation anxiety for even the most comfortable infants because of the presence of numerous other adults and infants. Although most infants are able to maintain themselves comfortably in this situation by visual and vocal contact with their mothers, with only occasional tactile reunions, Malcolm and his mother were always together as he leaned or sat against her or pulled her about the room by her fingers or skirt hem. He allowed no one else to touch him. His mother usually gave in to his constant demands immediately, although every now and then her intense irritability and anger broke through and she burst into tears. She would then leave the nursery with Malcolm for the day.

Malcolm gradually developed an unusual way of coping with his anxiety about being in the nursery. Leaving the nursery room itself with his mother in tow, he would walk through the hallways, touching certain places and objects in a regular fixed sequence. As his anxiety in the nursery gradually began to abate, the sequence of these walks began to change. He relinquished his mother's hand, greeted and waved at strangers, abandoned his routine of tactile behaviors, and played peek-a-boo games with his mother.

Malcolm's dawning independence from his mother was paralleled by his growing interest in one of our nursery books which contained a picture of a bear. Looking at the picture became his favorite nursery pastime. At the same time his mother reported that he had begun to wrap his legs tightly about his bear as he fell asleep at night, that he insisted the bear be near him during the day and that it be replaced in his crib before he left the house each morning.

The thrust of his individuation brought with it, however, an increase in hostile aggression. He threw balls at children and mothers in the nursery and bit his mother's shoulder. Part of the anger was directed against himself, for he began to gag himself, often to the point of actual regurgitation. His mother responded to his new independence and hostile aggression with corresponding anger and increasing withdrawal from her son.

Malcolm's development of awareness of his anal, urinary, and genital areas and functions proceeded in the following manner: Following his lip injury at 13½ months, the intense genital manipulation abated after a few weeks, returning to its former level and quality. Then at 15 months, just when Malcolm entered our nursery, he began to hold his penis during his bath, and for the first time this was accompanied by sounds of pleasure and enjoyment. At 15½ months he squatted and peered down at his penis. At 17 months he squeezed its tip and urinated immediately afterward. Then he began to lie prone, with his legs tightly wrapped around his bear, and rhythmically rubbed his perineal area up and down against the bear in unmistakable erotic masturbation.

He was concurrently more aware of his urinary functioning. At 17 months he engaged in intense water play in the nursery after he had urinated on the floor at home in the morning. He produced "puddles" of juice and milk on the floor, playing in these as he played in his urinary puddles. He manipulated the family garden hose endlessly, directing the stream and intently examining the nozzle. He also held long objects such as pretzel sticks in the faucet stream and then sucked on them. He also sucked the tail of a newly acquired stuffed tiger. But there was a hint of what was to follow when Malcolm adamantly refused to use broken pretzels for his faucet game.

In contrast to most of the male infants in our research sample, Malcolm's anal-zone awareness emerged simultaneously with his urinary and phallic awareness. (Anal awareness ordinarily became evident in the boys sometime between 12 and 14 months, and urinary and phallic awareness appeared several months later.) When Malcolm deposited a stool on the kitchen floor one day, he insisted that it remain there for some time while he examined and touched it, unlike other infants in our group. A bout of afebrile diarrhea culminated in several more stool "accidents" on the carpet. Placing his bear, Boo, on a potty chair at home, a device he himself had never been encouraged to use, he pretended to wipe its perineum. He also attempted to wipe his mother's perineum with toilet paper as she sat on the toilet, a behavior she permitted.

Play reflections of Malcolm's anal concerns appeared in the form of his rushing to turn light switches on and off whenever he heard the toilet being flushed. He also played endlessly with the family vacuum cleaner and its parts, repeatedly detaching and attaching them. This preoccupation betrayed not only his anal concerns but also his anxiety about phallic intactness. Although his play was now more varied and generally freer in quality, he began to avoid certain situations which appeared to be related to concern over the genital difference. As already mentioned, he would no longer accept broken pretzels for his faucet game. Small sores on his fingers were now a source of some distress. But above all, he began to retreat from his mother and turn toward his father, a shift that culminated in a dramatic scene during his 18th month when he refused to go home with his mother after a nursery session.

This episode was followed over the next few weeks by a sudden and severe upsurge in hostile aggressive behavior toward his mother, during the course of which he bit her several times and pinched her breasts, although he also clung to her in a whining and demanding fashion. However, the biting was soon displaced to his bear, Boo, as well as a host of other inanimate objects in the nursery and at home, including furniture and toys. The mobilization of this defensive displacement served to protect his relationship with his mother to some degree. Although his appetite increased at the same time, he refused to eat any food that was cut up or broken, so intense was his castration anxiety, and he gagged himself repeatedly as his anger became partially self-directed. Finally, his rage culminated in several full-scale temper tantrums.

Malcolm became even more attached to his bear as this hostile upheaval continued, but he now also required his stuffed tiger, the tail of which he used for sucking. Malcolm's rage and distress were mirrored by his mother who clung to him even as she angrily told him that he must learn to be on his own. And for the first time she hit him and admitted that she felt utterly helpless in dealing with him. The father, who was soon caught up in the angry whirl, suddenly decided to shift Malcolm from his crib to a bed "in order to get him ready for the new baby." Malcolm spent one sleepless night in the bed and the next day clung to his mother even more tenaciously. He demanded food, then threw it back at her and, instead, took out of her purse a small bottle containing one of her cosmetics. After holding this tightly clutched in his fist all day, he smashed it to bits on the floor when he was forced to remain alone without his mother for a short while that afternoon. Perhaps this was the first of a long line of fetishistic objects to which he subsequently became attached.

With this rapid and dramatic deterioration in Malcolm's relationship with his mother, his attachment shifted almost completely to his father. He called for his father in preference to his mother, wept bitterly whenever his father left him, and asked for his father's possessions, particularly his pens. When these were refused him, he managed to obtain a pen belonging to his nursery observer, and as he scribbled with it he was overheard murmuring, "Daddy, Daddy."

When Malcolm was returned to his crib after the one night's separation from it, he greeted his animals, told his parents to go away, and now initiated an entirely new type of play in which his bear was the central character and humans played no part. He spent hours arranging the animals and talking to them, sat Boo in his own potty chair, tried to bathe the bear, and refused to eat unless Boo was seated next to him so that Malcolm could feed him. He often insisted that Boo be taken on family outings, "talked" to the bear whenever his parents talked to one another, and one day wrapped his mother's scarf about Boo's neck. He also insisted at this time that he be allowed to carry his mother's pocketbook over his arm, just as she did. The bear had apparently become an important substitute object for his mother, but one which also had a phallic quality, as we shall see. This denial of the genital difference was further fortified by his assertion of the presence of the female phallus — the pocketbook he draped over himself in identification with his phallic mother.

Malcolm had become attached to one of the bears in the nursery, which he also called Boo. During one nursery session he indicated that he wanted this bear to be undressed, but was told that the bear's clothes could not be removed. He then proceeded to lie upon the bear, kissing it in an unmistakably erotic fashion, and squeezing it between his thighs. Now, whenever he became distressed in the nursery, he sought out the picture-book teddy bear instead of his mother. Furthermore, by the end of his 19th month, Malcolm was using his bear at home for open and vigorous masturbation against his naked genitals, a behavior with which his parents did not interfere. By 20 months this masturbation was accompanied by erections, and a facial expression of arousal and pleasure. But he also bit the bear, and was found to have swallowed a good deal of the fuzzy covering, an all-too-clear reflection of the sado-masochistic nature of this attachment.

As the time for his mother's delivery approached, Malcolm's attachment to his father became even more intense. At times he insisted on bringing one of his father's socks or his furry hat to the nursery, and imitated his father's every behavior, including urinating into the toilet in the upright position. (He had by this time acquired the names for the male and female genitals, differentiating them quite correctly.)

Reviewing Malcolm's development after he entered our nursery, we see that the impact of the nursery, with its implied threat of separation, had resulted in a marked increase in his anxiety. Malcolm's separation and individuation from his mother were of course quite atypical and unduly influenced by his rage at her. His investment in the bear, not only in the flesh, so to speak, but also in its pictorial image, could only serve as a less than satisfactory substitute. Furthermore, as his awareness of the genital difference increased, so did his castration anxiety, and he not only hugged and carried the bear next to his chest, but also held it in contact with his genital area. This new use of the bear coincided with the masturbatory type of genital behavior he now showed for the first time. Whereas his earlier genital play had consisted solely of tactile contact, beginning at 15½ months he looked at his penis as he touched it and experimented with it. Furthermore, much of the play behavior of this period—his interest in the garden hose, the stick pretzels, and the vacuum-cleaner tubing—reflected his preoccupation with his genital zone. A new level of awareness of the genital area itself had been attained, and genital-zone derivative play and curiosity had emerged for the first time, indicating the onset of the early genital phase. His use of the bear for masturbation probably represented at this time an attempt to reproduce actively the sensations that had been aroused passively during his early physical intimacy with his parents' bodies.

Then, in the midst of this very active period of genital exploration and masturbation, evidence of increasing castration anxiety began to appear—undue concern over small sores, refusal of broken pretzels, anxious examination of the perineal area of his mother's body and his animals, and, later on, his refusing to eat broken or cut food.

The intensified massive castration anxiety in turn began to revive his barely latent fears of anal as well as object loss. In contrast to the relatively calm period of Malcolm's 15th to 17th months, his rage was now explosive. As his hostile ambivalence toward his mother increased, whining and clinging to her even as he bit her and refused to go home with her, he not only turned to his father, but was also propelled into greater and greater involvement with his bear and tiger, as if to protect his mother from his rage at her. However, even this inanimate world was invaded by his erotized aggression, for he bit the very animals he loved so dearly.

The explosive rage was probably derived from several sources. His mother's increasing preoccupation with her advancing pregnancy posed a further threat to an already highly ambivalent relationship. A major increment, however, seemed to be derived from his growing awareness of the genital difference with its enormous threat of castration to a child whose basic sense of body integrity had already received so many grave insults.

The removal of his crib must have constituted just enough additional jeopardy to his wavering sense of his object world to force him to turn even more to the inanimate world of his animals. The temporary loss of his crib also seemed to provoke an additional increment of castration as well as object-loss anxiety, which were reflected in a new series of behaviors—his requiring his mother's cosmetic bottle and her scarf and bag to support his own seriously threatened sense of genital intactness as well as to assert the presence of his mother and her phallus.

It was at this time that Malcolm turned decisively toward his father, using his father's concrete possessions as further support of his own sense of phallic integrity. This relationship was a far less ambivalent one than with the mother and did help Malcolm in his extremely agitated state. However, although he began to be more comfortable once more, this was clearly at the cost of a relative withdrawal from the world of reality. His play with his menagerie of stuffed animals was intense and obligatory, and it served as a partial defense against the triple anxieties of object loss, self-disintegration, and castration.

Following the birth of a sibling when he was slightly over 21 months of age, Malcolm's anger at both mother and sibling became even more intense, and there was increasing evidence of massive anxiety concerning general body intactness, object loss, and castration. He played endlessly with vacuum cleaner parts, insisting upon taking pieces of the stiff tubing to bed with him, wore his mother's scarf, slept in a prone position with his hands folded over his genitals, and had a series of nightmares. Malcolm verbalized his anxiety about castration, body disintegration, and object loss in unmistakable terms during this period. He expressed his fear that his penis, his arms, and his legs would come off and that his mother would go away and not come back. And for the first time, he attempted to rub his penis directly against his mother's body when masturbating.

When Malcolm was just two years old, his baby sister died unexpectedly, an event that precipitated Malcolm's use of a whole cluster of new inanimate objects, all of which seemed to possess infantile fetishistic qualities. Increased masturbation with his bear was now combined with direct manual masturbation, and he slept with his bear and his old blue blanket held between his thighs, surrounded by an assortment of other stuffed animals. Anal masturbation and smearing began shortly thereafter, along with an episode of stool retention and nighttime soiling, and Malcolm's fears spread to include water, dogs, horses, and haircuts.

Malcolm's early life was an extraordinarily difficult one, with its numerous traumatic events and family tragedies. We shall try to trace the course of development which eventually resulted in such a serious disturbance in object relations and the confusion in sexual identity, trends which appeared to have taken a decisive pathological turn during the period of anal, urinary, and genital awareness, at about 15 to 16 months. For it was at this time that erotization of aggression emerged and his use of inanimate objects began to deviate decisively from the normal pattern.

The early peculiar relationships with both parents had resulted in considerable delay in separation and individuation, as well as premature genital arousal during the first year. With the cumulative trauma of the separation at eight months, the family move, the mother's new pregnancy, and the injury to the crucial oral area at 13 months, with its subsequent interference in oral gratification, there was a rise in hostile aggression and a channeling of tension through the precociously activated genital pathway. A greater reliance on the partially animate world of his transitional objects served to allay some of his anxiety over both object and anal loss at that time. Although the genital pathway served for the premature discharge of excessive tension, this zone had not yet attained its maturational level as an erotogenic zone from which pleasure could be derived.

Convoyed by his animals and by his growing attachment to his father, Malcolm was able to advance toward greater separation and individuation until the period of the early genital phase at 15 to 16 months. Unfortunately, this coincided with his mother's increasing withdrawal from him. As he became more aware of the genital difference, his castration anxiety mounted and his earlier fears of body disintegration and object loss were intensified. Massive rage interfered even more with the maternal relationship, and his fury contaminated his emerging genitality. A sadomasochistic behavioral pattern slowly emerged, clearly reminiscent of the reconstructive material described by Bak (1968) in connection with his adult patients with sadomasochistic perversions and bisexual identification.

It was during this period of intensifying castration anxiety that Malcolm's use of inanimate objects began to have a definitely fetishistic character. His need for his mother's cosmetic bottle, scarf, and bag bore testimony to his wavering sense of genital intactness, his beginning feminine identification, and his attempts to assert the presence of the female phallus.

We have already described infants who began to utilize inanimate objects other than the usual transitional objects in an unusual manner during this early period of concern over the genital difference at about 16 to 19 months (see Chapter 10). In agreement with

Greenacre's (1970) formulation, we have come to regard these particular objects as infantile fetishes. In the context of a developing preoedipal castration reaction, the infantile fetish seems to emerge when there is a significant increment in aggression, as if to bolster the wavering sense of body as well as phallic integrity through their firmness and durability. The firmness and durability seem to stand in contrast to the usual soft transitional object, the latter representing the positive and loving aspects of the infant's attachment to the mother.

Under normal circumstances children of this age use inanimate objects both as early representatives of external reality in the service of their developing sense of this reality and as external representatives of internal body sensations and states. But Malcolm (and children like him) seemed to utilize inanimate objects primarily for the satisfaction of his own narcissistic needs rather than in relation to any objective attributes they possessed. The attachment to these objects served to bolster his faltering sense of his own body and phallus and also to assert the presence of the female phallus.

The overwhelming castration anxiety, an outgrowth of the earlier interference with body schematization as well as his disturbed object ties, occurred precisely in connection with his developing awareness of the sexual difference and his own sexual identity. The confusion in sexual identity resulted from the disruption of his earlier symbiotic relationship to his mother, with its attendant escalation in hostile aggression, the subsequent erotization of aggression, and the lack of a firm enough identification with his father.

Malcolm's struggle to maintain his denial of female

castration came to occupy much of his psychological energy as he summoned up the various defensive measures described. Nonetheless, the denial periodically broke down. We believe this struggle stemmed from his early highly ambivalent, hostile, but intensely symbiotic tie to his mother and a genital identification with her which had never really been surrendered. For despite his discovery of the genital difference toward the end of his second year, this infant seemed unable to make a firm identification of himself as a boy. His continued attempts to resolve this uncertainty certainly brought no real or lasting conviction, and his sense of sexual identity probably remained a substantially feminine one at its core throughout the period of our contact with him.

We subsequently learned that a brief period of psychotherapy during Malcolm's third year was terminated by the parents when Malcolm was three years and two months of age. At that time, he was acutely fearful of any separation from his mother, with whom he was at the same time intensely provocative and angry. He was afraid of being alone with his father or other people, had smeared feces and urine on several occasions, stuttered, and suffered from a marked sleep disturbance. His attachment to his inanimate objects was as intense as ever. He could not tolerate anything broken, he frequently verbalized his fear of castration, he protected his genitals with his hands, and he refused to use the feminine pronouns or to acknowledge their use by others.

CHAPTER 13

GENITAL-DRIVE
DEVELOPMENT IN
THE SECOND YEAR

Because our direct observations were confined to the infant's second year of life and the latter part of the first year, we have had to rely on the parents' reports for events leading up to this period. What we learned, however, confirmed Freud's remarks on infantile genitality, as well as the findings of subsequent investigators in this area. Freud (1905), in discussing infantile masturbation, noted that the mother's various caretaking activities, as well as accidental stimulation of the genital zone, stimulate pleasurable feelings during infancy. These experiences, he said, lay the foundation for the future primacy of the genital zone. Freud noted that the masturbation of early infancy seems to disappear after "a short time," but may persist without interruption until puberty. A second phase of masturbation, according to Freud, consisted of the revival of the sexual instinct belonging to the genital zone and took place some time after infancy, usually before the fourth year. Freud also (1931) remarked on the possibility that little girls might masturbate less frequently and less energetically than little boys.

Spitz and Wolf (1949) investigated the "masturbation" of early infancy in their classic study of the auto-erotic practices of infants whose mothers were confined to institutions. They found a definite correlation between the quality of the infants' relationship with the mother during the first year and the emergence of auto-erotic behavior. Only those infants who had established a tie to the mother of good-enough quality developed genital autoerotic practices, a finding later supported by Provence and Lipton's (1962) work with infants in institutions.

Our own data throw light on some of Spitz and Wolf's original descriptions. We learned, through retrospective accounts offered by the parents of our infants, that the boy usually discovers his penis during bathing or diapering—a situation of intimacy and passive caretaking with the mother. The average age of penile discovery preceded the girls' initial genital discovery by one to three months. The initial genital discovery was followed, in both sexes, by many episodes of casual touching and intermittent self-handling of the genitals during the next few months.

This early genital play corresponds with that described by Kleeman (1971, 1975) in the five children on whom he reported. The nature of this early genital play may be summarized as follows. Boys and girls show a difference not only in time of onset but in the quality of early genital play as well. The girls' play is less persistent, less focused, less frequent, and seems less intentional than the boys'. We think this difference is probably due to the more direct mechanical stimulation by diapers and cleansing which is experienced by the boy not only because of the greater exposure of his genitals, but also because of the presence of erections from birth onward. Differences in parental handling probably also contribute to boy/girl variations.

Toward the end of the first year, the ego capacity of intentionality began to emerge at about the same time as intentional reaching for the penis occurred quite regularly in the boys, an event that correlated with the attainment of upright posture. This new intentional penile grasping was often accompanied by definite evidence of pleasurable nonerotic affect. Whereas the infant of six months played with his toes, fingers, and body in a generally exploratory, more passive fashion, the 12-month-old actively and intentionally examined his body parts in a new way. He compared his own facial features with his mother's by pointing at and touching them, and soon this comparison included the rest of his body as he proceeded in a regular sequence from facial features in a cephalocaudad direction. Erections were not noted in connection with the early genital handling, but they did appear whenever the male infant was about to urinate, evidently under the pressure of a full bladder.

Spitz's later report (1962) and Kleeman's (1965) report on a mother's observation of her infant son's developing genital self-stimulation agree that this early genital play is primarily an aspect of body discovery. Although Kleeman noted that a mild to moderate degree of erotic pleasure was present during the genital self-stimulation, the infant was not self-absorbed nor was there evidence of mounting arousal. Following the child into his second year, Kleeman (1966) found that the infant's awareness of penile sensation had increased, along with an increase in total genital sensitivity, which appeared by about 15 months. Kleeman considered both phenomena transitional between the body exploratory genital behavior of the first year and the definitively masturbatory stimulation of the oedipal years. We agree that the genital play of the first year is, under normal circumstances, in the nature of general body exploration and cannot yet be considered true masturbation.

ANAL-PHASE ORGANIZATION

The intimate relationship between the development of psychosexual organization and object relations was reflected around the beginning of the second year, in most of the infants we studied, in the concurrent appearance of acute separation anxiety and reflections of anal-phase organization. One boy, whose separation and individuation were somewhat precocious and whose toilet training was initiated at 10 months of age, began to demonstrate his anal awareness at that time, while another boy, whose relationship with his mother was particularly passive and who was slower to separate and individuate, did not indicate anal awareness until his 16th month.

Although most of the mothers had not yet begun to toilet-train their infants, both boys and girls began to show a regularly occurring increase in negativism and ambivalence, along with direct anal-zone awareness and also anal-derivative play some time between their 12th and 14th month. Mahler's studies of the separation-individuation process (Mahler et al., 1975) have revealed glimpses of anal-phase-related behaviors, along with ample evidence of the emotional ambivalence and negativism that is so characteristic of object relations during the anal phase. Kestenberg (1968) has identified rhythmic body patterns during the second year, which she considers characteristic of anal-zone functioning.

In our own material, the richness and complexity of anal-phase behavior seemed to indicate that a new level of psychological organization had indeed been attained. In every instance, anal-derivative behavior appeared only after anal-zone awareness was already present; and fears of anal loss emerged subsequent to anal-derivative behavior, these fears usually reaching their peak intensity near the middle of the second year.

At the anal zone itself, anal-phase emergence is marked by variations in bowel patterning, a decrease in frequency of bowel movements, a change in their consistency, the occurrence of diarrhea or constipation, and such behaviors as squatting, flushing, straining, and grunting, accompanying or directly preceding defecation. Following the completion of defecation, the infant might either signal for or begin to resist diaper change, but there was definite interest now in the stool itself and in exploring the anal area. The infants also began to use gestures and words supplied by the parent for the act of defecation and its product.

Further phase-related changes were the bouts of directed aggression and ambivalence about which the mothers began to complain, those drive-connected affects which were identified by Freud (1905) as characteristic of the anal-phase organization. Ego reflections of this new level of organization included anal curiosity, as the infants investigated the anal areas in other people, in toy animals and dolls, and invented many play sequences in which the form, structure, or other attributes (such as an olfactory interest) resembles that of the anal area itself or the stool. Renewed interest in peek-a-boo games, collecting and piling games, and in-and-out games were still other examples of the enormous variety of play in which the anal-derivative influence was unmistakable. Furthermore, the toilet apparatus itself — the flushing mechanism, the lid, bowl, and water — were a never-ending source of interest, delight — and also of some anxiety — to the youngsters at this time.

URINARY AWARENESS

The richness of this aspect of our research data was particularly rewarding in view of the paucity of this type of material in the infant observational literature. In our infants, urinary-zone awareness emerged sometime between the 12th and 14th month in most instances — usually, although not always, after anal awareness was present and independent of attempts at toilet training. Urinary-derivative behavior followed soon afterward. Direct zonal manifestations included changes in urinary diurnal patterning and changes in behavior that either directly preceded, accompanied, or followed urination. The infants now paid selective attention to wet diapers; the girls would squat to look at and touch the urinary streams and the boys would handle the penis itself as well as the urinary stream as they experimented with interrupting and then resuming urination. Both boys and girls now liked to play in the puddles of urine they had produced. They became intensely curious about the urinary function in others — adults and peers and animals — and their play was now rich in many sequences involving pouring and squirting liquids, whether with faucets, hoses, watering cans, or the mouth. In all these forms of urinary-derivative behavior, the structural similarity to the urinary act itself was unmistakable.

Most of our small subjects, both boys and girls, succeeded in being admitted to observe the parents' toileting at this period of their development, in spite of parental modesty in several families. Particularly in the boys, the new excitement and exhibitionistic pride in urination was coupled with clearly discernible scoptophilic development. The intense urinary curiosity, again in the boys, then rapidly became enmeshed in the early genital curiosity which soon appeared. Once they became interested, both boys and girls tried to grasp and sometimes mouth the father's urinary stream. As far as we could determine, this behavior was not connected with an undue degree of parental exposure, but was simply an expression of the intense curiosity and interest evoked by a newly discovered phenomenon.

A decided difference was manifest between the boys and girls in their response to the mother's urination. The girls consistently clamored to be with the mother during her toileting, but the boys' interest was far more difficult to delineate. Some boys developed curiosity about the mother's urination even before the father's, but many of the boys seemed to avoid it altogether. We think that the boy's interest in the mother's urination rapidly becomes intertwined with the emerging awareness of the genital anatomical difference, and that this awareness promotes the development of a defensive denial in relation to the mother's perineum.

We were especially impressed by the parental reactions to their infant's urinary curiosity and exploration. The young child's natural impulse to explore the rather awesome spectacle of the male urinary stream by both oral and tactile measures aroused considerable uneasiness in even our most psychologically sophisticated fathers. Some continued to allow occasional touching, while others rapidly banished the little girl from the bathroom during their urination, although she was permitted to re-enter during bathing, showering, and shaving. The need to repress the erotic feelings aroused in the parent by the primitive childish curiosity is most striking. In several instances, within a week or two, many parents had forgotten all about the very information they themselves had offered. This tendency to repress such erotic reactions seems to be greater on the part of the father vis-à-vis his little daughter than it is between mother and son.

EMERGENCE OF GENITAL-PHASE ORGANIZATION

With increasing self-object differentiation at the beginning of the second year, the anal and urinary zones become heightened sources of pleasure and, at the same time, sources of anxiety as well; stool and urine are gradually invested not only with psychological significance as body parts which can be lost, but also seem to represent some aspect of the object (mother). This appears to apply especially to the stool, for anal loss is now almost invariably associated with some degree of anxiety. It is in the midst of the anal-urinary elaboration that genital self-stimulation of a qualitatively different variety emerged for the first time in our infants.

Sometime between the 15th and 19th months in the nontraumatized girls and boys we studied, the heightened genital sensitivity began to serve as a source of focused pleasure which was far more intense than the earlier forms of genital self-stimulation had provided. During the early weeks of this increased genital activity, both boys and girls carried on repetitive intense genital self-stimulation, either manually or by such indirect means as straddling objects, rocking, and thigh pressure. Both boys and girls attempted visual exploration of their genitals, in addition to the tactile genital contact. The accompanying erotic arousal included facial expressions of excitement and pleasure, flushing, rapid respiration, and perspiration. In the boys, masturbation was largely manual, penile erections were often part of the genital excitation — although these often occurred at other times as well — and the testicles were often included in the self-stimulation. The infant frequently made affectionate gestures and touched the mother's body during or subsequent to the genital self-stimulation.

At this time of life and in our culture, free access to the genitals is provided primarily during bathing and diapering, and it was during these times that masturbation was most common. Probably an additional factor accounting for the masturbation at these times was the infant's memory of earlier genital sensations during the countless maternal caretaking activities, as Freud (1933) pointed out.

In the girls, the new quality of genital self-stimulation observed consisted of manual, repetitive rubbing, squeezing, and pinching of the labia at the areas of the mons and clitoris. Because the genital area is so small at this age, it is usually impossible to determine whether the vaginal opening is stimulated at the same time. However, several of the mothers reported that the little girl's finger had actually been introduced into the opening of the vagina itself, although this was not the main site of stimulation.

In both sexes, open affectionate behavior to the mother as an accompaniment of the new genital self-stimulation began to disappear after the first few weeks and was soon replaced by the familiar inward gaze and a self-absorbed look. This development would seem to indicate that a fantasy feeling-state had now become a regular concomitant of the genital self-stimulation and that this new type of genital activity is true masturbation. Furthermore, various forms of nonverbal yet clearly symbolic behavior accompanied the new genital activity, suggesting the presence of some concurrent, albeit rudimentary, fantasy state. For example, many of the little girls in our study used nursing bottles, transitional-object blankets, stuffed animals, and dolls for direct masturbatory contact. We think it likely that this early fantasy formation includes a partial memory of the earlier maternal contact, since the genital manipulation so often involves these typical "mother-me" objects. Concrete objects are then gradually discarded, and masturbation approaches the adult model, although some people never relinquish concrete objects entirely (Greenacre, 1969).

The emergence of genital-derivative behavior in all our infants who were developing normally followed the emergence of true masturbation. This genital-derivative behavior could be traced in almost every sector of the infant's functioning, whether in the sphere of object relations or in some aspect of the many nascent ego functions. The boys showed a definite increase in their use of phallic-shaped toys — cars, trucks, airplanes — and other objects which could be put into motion during the early weeks of the early genital phase. Furthermore, the strutting body posture and phallic pride of the boys was in sharp contrast to the flirtatiousness of the girls, who lifted their skirts and exposed their genitals. In contrast to the boys, the girls' genital-derivative behavior almost immediately became caught up in their reaction to the genital differences. Girls used inanimate objects to replace the missing phallus at the pubic area in themselves and other females, as well as the usual anatomically incomplete dolls and toy animals. The gestures and words they used clearly indicated that both boys and girls were now aware of the genital anatomical difference.

During the early weeks of the early genital phase, masturbation was displaced transiently to umbilicus, anus, ears, or other parts of the body. In the girls, doll play increased remarkably and the quality of the play itself changed in that dolls were continually undressed, the crotch area examined, phallic-shaped objects were placed at this area, and the dolls themselves were often used for masturbation or were placed beneath the genital area at bedtime. Many girls then adopted one of the dolls as an obligatory companion, needed during both waking and sleeping hours.

As the signs of specific endogenous genital responsiveness mounted, the curiosity about the sexual difference emerged in both boys and girls. In boys, erections now frequently followed their genital handling, and they also appeared in response to the mother's genital stimulation. The increased sexual curiosity soon led to visual comparisons that the toddlers made: the boys stared at the father's penis and then at their own during those increasingly frequent times when both were naked together either in the shower or during the father's toileting. The curiosity also led both boys and girls to try to see and touch their mother's breasts and to peer beneath the skirts of women and dolls.

At about 16 or 17 months, all the girls in our sample, even those who had not witnessed their parents' toileting previously, now succeeded in being allowed into the bathroom with their parents. Those who had earlier seen their fathers urinating now began to show interest in the penis for the first time. Curiosity quickly spread to other aspects of body differences, such as hair and clothing.

Discovery of the Sexual Anatomical Difference

With the emergence of curiosity about the sexual difference, the reactions of most of the boys and those of the girls definitely diverged. Initially, both boys and girls appeared to have a shocklike reaction which consisted of a rather ubiquitous denial of the genital difference, with displacement of interest to the mother's breasts, umbilicus, and buttocks. Virtually all the girls then went on to develop preoedipal castration reactions, which included a recrudescence of their recently allayed fears of object loss and self-disintegration as well as a variety of other regressive symptoms, depending upon the severity of their reaction. But there were also developmental advances in most of the girls in the form of more elaborate fantasy play and early attempts at graphic representation. While this may have represented to some degree the use of denial through fantasy, the new developments also reflected the girls' defensive efforts to cope with the anxiety provoked by the recognition of the genital difference.

The recognition of the genital difference in all of the girls led to a definite heightening of the already present ambivalence of anal-phase development and the simultaneous emergence of a new erotic and flirtatious interest in the father in all but a very small number of the girls in our sample. We view this erotic turn to the father as an important preparatory step for the positive oedipal attachment soon to appear. This earlier erotic turn contains, however, no oedipal resonance, for the girl gives no sign of jealousy with regard to the mother; the relation among the three is still dyadic, not triadic, in nature.

The eight girls in our sample who developed intense preoedipal castration reactions had all experienced an important threat to either the developing body image or their maternal relationship during their first year. It is evident that the girls were far more vulnerable than the boys to the effect of observing the anatomical difference. Their preoedipal castration reactions affected almost every area. At the genital zone itself, manual masturbation was frequently replaced by indirect stimulation. Some girls abandoned masturbation entirely, while several continued to masturbate, but without pleasure. In several instances we observed distinct signs of shame and embarrassment in some of the girls during their 15th to 18th months when urine trickled down their thighs, leaving puddles which clearly made them uncomfortable. Since this reaction was confined to the girls, we think it is related to the dawning awareness of the anatomical differences.

Furthermore, those girls who had previously differentiated boy from girl verbally now frequently confused the two, and use of the word "boy" often dropped out altogether.

It was in the area of genital-derivative behavior that the difference between the sexes was most impressive. The girls showed a far greater tendency to use regressive oral and anal comforting measures, including mouthing and sucking, anal masturbation, and anal and urinary retention; displacement of masturbation to other body parts was most common. Oral- and anal-phase anxieties of object and anal loss were intensified and were now reflected in renewed fears of separation, while the castration anxiety itself gave rise to intense concern over small body imperfections (minor bruises and scratches) and the avoidance of broken toys of any kind.

The changes in the form of masturbation, or its

total inhibition in some little girls, are due to their efforts to deny the sexual difference by means of temporarily avoiding the whole genital area — an avoidance which soon disintegrates as sexual pressure rises. Nor can the girl continue to deny her own genital anatomy without threatening her developing sense of reality.

The castration reactions in the girls ranged from mildly transitory or moderate ones to severe reactions which resulted in profound disruptions affecting almost every aspect of behavior.

We believe these castration responses to the sexual difference are organizing influences in the life of the girl from this time onward and that they determine the direction of much of her subsequent psychosexual development in both enhancing and inhibiting directions, as well as other aspects of her personality. Perhaps it is in its effect upon developing object ties that the effect of the castration reaction in girls is most striking. While both boys and girls had developed a special relationship with the father toward the end of the first year, as part of their growing sense of separateness from the mother, it was in the midst of their castration reactions that most of the girls made the erotic turn to the father, seeking out the mother only at times of distress. These were the girls who had had a relatively successful experience during their first year. However, where the earlier relationship with the mother had been of poor quality, or if the girl had suffered important bodily trauma during her first year or had experienced the birth of a sibling during the second part of the second year, hostile dependence upon the mother was enormously aggravated in the wake of the discovery of the sexual anatomical difference.

We believe that these early events in the psychosexual sphere exert a decisive influence upon the developing libidinal attachment to the father in these little girls, determining whether a definitive erotic shift toward the father takes place toward the end of the second year, or whether the tie to the mother persists and becomes intensified and even more ambivalent. Whether the shift to the father takes place will, as we have said, influence the character of the subsequent oedipal phase. The milder castration reaction would appear to facilitate the girl's turn to the father as her new love object with a continuing, albeit less intense attachment to her mother, while the more profound castration reaction would be expected to lead to a predominantly negative oedipal constellation with the choice of the mother as the primary but ambivalently loved object.

Finally, we noted the occurrence of mood changes in many girls which have occurred concurrently with their preoedipal castration reactions. Mahler (1966) described the sadness, the loss of zest and enthusiasm, in many of the little girls she described during the same chronological period, a change in mood which she had attributed to the rapprochement crisis and which seems to be of greater severity in little girls than in little boys. We believe that these mood changes, which may range from very mild reactions to the establishment of a basic depressive mood seen in one of the girls in our study (see Chapter 5), can probably best be identified as reflecting developments in both the psychosexual and object-relations spheres.

We have seen that the symbolic function in girls

advances in complexity under the impact of the preoedipal castration reaction. It is in connection with
these preoedipal castration reactions, for example, that
many girls develop a special type of attachment to dolls
or other inanimate objects, an attachment different
from the earlier type of doll play in that the dolls and
other objects serve as "infantile fetishes" in support of
the wavering sense of sexual identity. Broken toys are
avoided, and the girls begin to use crayons, pens, and
pencils at this time, earlier than most of the boys in our
group, in an early but definite attempt at graphic representation.

In contrast to this expansion of play in many of the
girls, however, those who suffered the most intense castration reactions suffered a considerable constriction in
their fantasy life in that imaginative play of all types
became sparse and stereotyped. This went hand in hand
with a restriction in their general intellectual curiosity:
their exploration of the world about them became
definitely narrower in scope.

We have made such detailed observations of the
early semisymbolic play of our subjects precisely because it is during the second year that the critical transition between semisymbolic communication and early
forms of verbal communication normally occurs.

In contrast to the girls, the boys seemed far less
overtly disturbed by their discovery of the anatomical
difference. All but four of the boys showed only a minimal degree of overt reaction to this discovery. We think
that this apparent lack of overt disturbance can be
ascribed to the boy's continued attempts to deny the

sexual difference, a denial which can be supported by his avoidance of confrontation with his mother's genitals and with those of his female peers, and by the boy's turn toward the father in nonerotic identification with him. (See Freud, 1921, p. 105.)

We noted a brief upsurge of masturbation in the boy, lasting only a month or so, and then a decline of direct manual masturbation, together with a definite increase in the level of their motor activities. We believe that both of these latter developments reflect the boy's anxiety in relation to the recognition of the genital difference, with its implied threat of castration and regression to the more symbiotic type of passive attachment to the mother.

From time to time, the boys' denial of the genital difference broke down, and evidence of anal-genital confusion emerged. Any attempts at toilet training met with strong objection for a period until the anal-genital confusion once again subsided. At these times, there were also renewed regressive requests for the bottle and increased attachment to transitional objects. Heightened anxiety over separation recurred, and furthermore, the boys tended to avoid witnessing the mother's genitals and her urination. Some of the boys had shown an interest in phallic types of play with cars and trucks by 15 or 16 months, or even earlier, but there was a definite increase in the intensity of this play, as well as the rough-and-tumble play with the father as the paternal identification progressed. However, the fantasy play was far less elaborate than in the girl.

FURTHER FINDINGS

As we observed earlier (see Chapter 3), we found

ourselves paying less and less attention to the distinction we had originally made between the randomly selected and preselected infants because of the unusual first-year experiences of the randomly selected that came to light during the course of each year of our research. In this summary of our findings, therefore, we must include infants from both groups.

Our original postulate stated that all infants would show evidence of passage through an early genital phase sometime between 15 and 24 months of age. This condition was satisfied in all 66 subjects, except that the time of onset was several months earlier in most and several months later in others, where unusual circumstances prevailed. We also assumed that circumstances that interfered with the developing sense of body intactness or with the mother-child relationship would affect the way in which the infant experienced the early genital phase. This condition was also satisfied.

What we did not anticipate was the difference between the randomly selected male and female infants in their reactions to perceiving the anatomical difference between the sexes. Our greatest surprise was in connection with the nature and paucity of the overt castration reactions in the boys. Of the 23 boys in our randomly selected group, although about a dozen, as we later learned, had undergone a significant experience during their first year either in regard to body-image development or object relations, only five showed serious effects of these experiences. Two of the five had been excessively exposed to parental nudity and developed precocious genital awareness at the beginning of their second year. A third boy had suffered from a severe skin infection from his first to fifth months; a fourth boy wore leg braces from 11 to 14 months and had a particularly teasing, ambivalent relationship with his mother; and a fifth boy wore leg splints for several months early in his first year. (These boys were in our random group because the parents had neglected to mention these factors to us at the initial interview.) All five of these boys evidenced diffuse castration reactions toward the end of their second year, reactions that tended to emerge, disappear, and then re-emerge as they entered the third year. One boy, who was subjected to repair of a hernia at 21½ months, suffered an acute castration reaction postoperatively.

Yet another group of six boys among the randomly selected ones differed from the others in that the onset of the early genital phase did not occur until they were well beyond the beginning of their third year. The parents of one of these infants were emotionally extremely inhibited, especially with regard to sexuality; two other boys in this group were emotionally remote from their parents, who were having serious marital problems. The remaining three boys with delayed genitality were locked in an overly close and erotic relationship with their mothers, and two of them, we learned, developed moderately severe castration reactions during their third and fourth years and manifested some confusion in sexual identity, though not as severe as occurred in the preselected cases.

In contrast to our findings with the boys, all but three of the 25 randomly selected girls developed castration reactions, which varied in degree from very mild to moderately severe. The only girls who did not develop castration reactions during the period of observation in our nursery were three whose early genital-phase development was definitely delayed. One of these girls acquired a baby sister when she was only 17 months old and, although this infant made a remarkable accommodation through her intense identification with her mother's nurturing and caretaking of the new baby, it was at the cost of her capacity to enjoy her genitals as a special pleasure source until many months beyond the average. Another girl with similarly delayed genital-phase onset had shown precocious separation and individuation in relation to her emotionally detached mother during her first year. The third infant with delayed onset of genitality had been hospitalized at four months of age for an acute illness for several weeks.

Although the delayed genitality just described resulted from three different experiences, all led to a relative fixation to earlier modes of gratification through the oral and anal routes. The nature of the object relations was similar in each case in that none of these girls had successfully negotiated beginning autonomy from the mother and had not begun to turn to the father in an erotic way. We suspect that these girls may well have difficulties with regard to their sense of sexual identity.

Of the remaining 22 randomly selected girls, we discovered in retrospect that 15 had earlier had a physical illness or body trauma or were suffering a disturbed relationship with the mother. Nine of these 15 girls did develop profound castration reactions. The traumatizations included four instances of rather severe maternal postpartum depressions, another mother's hospitalization for several weeks, and two instances where the infant had shown a definite preference for the father from the earliest months. This latter circumstance proved to have been a repetition of the mother's own experience as a child. This preference for the father was a serious blow to the mother's narcissism, resulting in severe disharmony between mother and child.

Further early predisposing factors in the randomly selected girls included an intensely exhibitionistic use of the girl by the mother (see Chapter 7), and two instances of urinary tract infections requiring catheterization and other diagnostic procedures.

The findings related to the preselected group of 10 boys were most surprising. Only three of these boys had severe overt castration reactions, two of whom we have described (see Chapters 4 and 12). The third, an adopted boy whose development in the first year was precocious in almost all sectors, developed an unusually early genital arousal during the latter part of his first year and a moderately severe castration reaction at the same time. In those boys in the preselected group in whom we could not discern a castration reaction, we did see definite distortions in the timing and quality of the early genital phase, and the developing sense of sexual identity was blurred. For example, four of these boys — two sets of twins — all of whom showed delay in separation and individuation, showed a similar delay in the emergence of the early genital phase. We were fortunate in being able to follow one set of twins into their third year and so could witness this delayed arousal. We can only assume it took place in the other set of twins, whom we were not able to observe further.

A boy with clubbed feet and a boy whose father

was away from home (see Chapter 4) developed severe and prolonged separation reactions. The early genital phases in both of these boys were shadowy in outline, the fear of object loss predominated over castration anxiety, and the attachment to the father was extremely attenuated in both cases. The sense of sexual identity in the twins, the boy with clubbed feet, and the boy whose father was away was shadowy.

The remaining three preselected male infants (one with leg casts and two with depressed mothers) all developed behavior indicating not only a shadowy but a confused sense of sexual identity during the latter part of their second year. Their major object of identification was the mother, although in each case the father lived at home with the family. Two of these boys engaged in transvestite behavior to a marked degree by the beginning of their third year, while the third boy showed a milder form of cross-dressing. In all three boys, although masturbation did emerge, the phallic quality of the masturbation itself and their genital derivative behavior was attenuated.

As already noted, the four boys whose castration reactions were intense all showed heightened aggressive ambivalence to the mother even as they became more closely attached to her and tended to identify with her rather than with the father. These boys showed an unusual pattern of response to their discovery of the genital difference. They clutched at their genitals when frustrated or upset — a reaction which seemed to serve for the discharge of aggression rather than as a source of pleasure.

Unlike the other boys in our sample, the semisymbolic play of these four boys developed quite elaborately and included the use of dolls and puppets. Yet the nature of the fantasy expression in these boys was quite different from the play elaboration seen in the girls as they dealt with their castration anxiety. Their play was rigid, repetitive, and compulsive, similar to the play of the girls with severe castration reactions. These boys reflected their maternal identification in their use of the mother's jewelry, clothes, cosmetics, and other possessions in "dress-up" in a way that seemed to forecast the development of a negative oedipal constellation.

CHAPTER 14

INFANTILE ORIGINS
OF SEXUAL IDENTITY

Although we did not set out to study the origins of the
sense of sexual identity as such, our findings inexorably
led us to that area. We agree with the *Glossary of Psychoanalytic Terms and Concepts* (Moore and Fine,
1968) that "The sense of identity begins with the child's
awareness that he exists as an individual in a world with
outer objects, and that he has his own wishes, thoughts,
and memories, and his own distinctive appearance."
We also agree that "sexual identity... usually represents
a predominant identification with the parent of the
same sex" (p. 50). We would amplify this definition by
saying that the primary core of this identification is
achieved at the time of the early genital phase and is
based on an early genital arousal that provides the basis
for the identification.

Much of the psychological development of the first

year or so is, of course, concerned with the establishment of a basic initial sense of the self and the other, as
Mahler's work has shown in such rich and remarkable
detail. Lichtenstein (1961) felicitously described the
process when he wrote that every mother lends shape to
an "identity theme" in her young infant, partially
through the feeding relationship which is apparently
different for boys and girls (see Murphy, 1962; Korner,
1973). Differences in early oral experiences of male and
female patients have been reported by Greenacre
(1950). Both Fraiberg (1972) and Kestenberg (1956,
1968) have stated that there is a close relationship between the oral and vaginal themes in the analytic material of their adult and child female patients. Furthermore, it is commonly observed that penile erections in
infant boys occur simultaneously with nursing, lending
further support to the well-known body plasticity of infants which allows early body sensations to be displaced
so readily from one area to another, particularly if these
areas are biologically predestined to provide sensuous
experience.

As Freud (1933, p. 20) stated, "the mother. . . by
her activities over the child's bodily hygiene inevitably
stimulated, and perhaps even roused for the first time
pleasurable sensations in her genitals." Kris (1951, p. 96)
elaborated on the primitive forerunners of later genitality when he wrote: "The transfer from general affection
to the genital zone itself. . . . may also arise as a consequence of the general bodily closeness to which, we assume, the child tends to react with sensation in the genital region." That the mother's activities are experienced
differently by boys and girls by virtue of their distinctive

genital anatomy, is well known. Analytic material from adult patients clearly illustrates how the specific sexual identity of the patient's child provokes unconscious fantasies in both parents, but particularly in the mother in the course of handling her infant's genitals during bathing, diapering, and other body ministrations. One has only to observe the repetitious intense genital cleaning practiced by some mothers in contrast to the almost complete avoidance of that area by others to be persuaded that the sexual fantasies aroused in the mother have a strong impact upon the infant.

Lichtenstein (1961, p. 47) describes the early mother-child interplay as "an interaction between two partners where each partner experiences himself as uniquely and specifically capable of serving as the instrument of the other's sensory gratification — such a partnership can be called a partnership of sensual involvement." Lichtenstein also (1961, p. 280) states, ". . . there is an innate body responsiveness, a capacity . . . to respond to contact with another person with a specific kind of somatic excitation which is not a drive, because it has no direction, but which is the innate prerequisite for the later development of a drive. . . . this responsiveness we may call sexual because it forms the matrix of later sexual development."

To the sensuous interactions just described, we would add the genital pressure of excitation transmitted from the adjacent anal and urinary areas, which contributes to a substantially different early body image for each sex.

An important contribution to the psychological study of early sexuality has been the work of Stoller

(1968, 1972) and his associates with a group Stoller has identified as transsexuals. Emphasizing the decisive influence of early parental rearing for the psychopathological disturbance he found in his small group of males, Stoller has described the beginnings of their feminine identification during their prephallic or preoedipal phases. Their mothers shared the common psychological feature of having treated their sons in a way that interfered with the development of "core gender identity" in the boys. Stoller does not entirely eliminate the contribution of either genital physiology or endocrinological and neurological factors to this particular failure to establish a basic sense of sexual identity.

In addition to his studies of transsexuals, Stoller has formulated a theory of feminine development. Postulating two phases of feminine development, he proposes that the second phase is added to the basic, original, primary one as a defensive device against the girl's growing awareness of the genital difference. Stoller's position here corresponds with that originally offered by Horney (1924, 1926), and supported by Jones (1927, 1933) and Zilboorg (1944), all of whom disagreed with Freud's view that the girl's feminine gender development began with the onset of the phallic phase. More recently, Fliegel (1973) has elaborated somewhat on Horney's and Jones' positions.

Another study of early sexuality has been carried out by Money and Ehrhardt (1972), who have been concerned with genetically and hormonally deviant individuals. Their findings suggest that it is the sex in which the infant is reared during the first two years of life that plays the major role in the establishment of gender identity. Their clinical data include material from several endocrinologically different groups of children. The first group consisted of genetically male individuals whose gonadal hormone was completely absent during the prenatal period. These infants, who were born with female-appearing external genitalia, developed along female lines if they were reared as females during the first 18 months of life—despite their genetic maleness. In contrast was a group of genetically female children who were hormonally androgenized during the prenatal period and who were also reared as girls. When studied during latency, their object choice was distinctly heterosexual and they regarded themselves as females, although they were "tomboyish" in that they preferred rough-and-tumble play and boys' toys instead of dolls. Money and Ehrhardt concluded from the study of these two groups that feminine gender identity is primarily dependent upon sex of rearing, rather than genetic endowment or prenatal gonadal hormones. The "tomboyishness" in the second group may have been due, the authors believe, to the minor influence of prenatal androgens.

A third group of infants, genetically male but with some prenatal hormonal androgen (rather than a complete absence of the prenatal androgen effect), were born with external genitalia of anomalous appearance. Several of these infants were reared as boys, and sex reassignment was attempted after the end of their second year, since the surgical reconstruction of adequate male genitalia is as yet unsatisfactory. These children suffered from a profound degree of psychological disturbance. Again, this experience points to the influence of postnatal factors in the human — in contrast to findings in lower species — in establishing gender identity. Money and Ehrhardt have designated the 18th month or so as the critical age beyond which successful sex reassignment is impossible. While these endocrinological and other biological studies have demonstrated that there are early sex differences in many areas of physical development, they have also highlighted the influence of object relations on sexual development. Furthermore, although biological factors undoubtedly influence developing psychological processes, the two phenomena are not necessarily parallel to one another.

In summary, the two most extensive studies of early sexual identity, those of Money and Ehrhardt, and of Stoller and his associates, have both identified the second half of the second year as a critical period for establishing gender identity. Although this period correlates chronologically with our findings, there is nonetheless some disagreement among us regarding the factors responsible for this critical period in gender development.

Our Findings

Subtle and perhaps not so subtle differences in parental handling of the infant during the first year or so, as described in the previous chapter, probably contribute to an incipient sense of sexual identity. But, aside from early self-stimulation patterns, it is only with the emergence of genital awareness — an endogenous precipitate of anal and urinary awareness — that differences between the boys and girls could be clearly discerned. It was the differences in the reaction to the awareness of the genital difference that seemed, above all, to mark the divergent paths each sex would take, a finding that strongly suggests that the second half of the second year of life is a critical period for the development of the sense of sexual identity. In the girls, this period was characterized by a remarkable increase in semisymbolic capacity and functioning in response to an almost universal castration reaction, and the recrudescence of fears of object loss and self-disintegration. The erotic turn to the father and a definite change in masturbatory patterns were further features which distinguished the sexual development in the girls. Although the girls appeared to be far more vulnerable than the boys in their development of intense penis envy and other castration-reaction phenomena, they also showed the advances in ego functioning already mentioned.

The boys, in contrast, showed far less overt disturbance as they defended against castration anxiety by a more profound denial and displacement. Furthermore, it was in connection with the development of exhibitionistic pride as well as the urinary technique or posture used by the boy that the degree of the father's availability and his emotional involvement with his son appeared to play an important role. In those families where the father was more available in general to his son, the father's interest in the boy's urinary progress and technique became an important aspect of their mutual involvement, and these boys tended to adopt the upright urinary posture some months before those whose fathers were less emotionally available to them or absent altogether. The importance of paternal availability and support for the boy's growing sense of his male sexual identity during the second part of the second year of life cannot be too strongly stressed. We believe it is a crucial factor in providing the boy with confirmation of his own phallic body image and allows him to eventually acknowledge the absence of a penis in his mother — a process which apparently extends over the next many months to the middle or even the end of the third year of life, according to some of our data.

The intensity of the boy's attachment to his mother diminished gradually in the boys in our group during the early genital phase, a change we believe to be a result of the profound if intermittent denial of the genital difference, and the boy's growing identification with the father. With the onset of the oedipal phase, however, the increase in genital-drive pressure tends to threaten the defenses built up during the course of the boy's initial reaction to his recognition of the genital difference. The new wave of erotic feeling toward the mother during the oedipal phase interferes with the boy's denial of the genital difference, while his rivalry with his father tends to obstruct the paternal identification. The upheaval of oedipal-phase development in the boy must represent a confluence of these various conflictual forces which were only partially and temporarily resolved during the early genital phase. The four boys who suffered from preoedipal castration reactions would be expected to experience a fragile oedipal phase, with a strong tendency to develop a negative oedipal attachment.

We believe the boy's extensive use of denial interferes with the capacity for symbolic elaboration in fantasy, in contrast to the girl. And above all, the boy's earlier sense of genital identification with his mother must be definitely disengaged at this critical juncture if he is to achieve a solid sense of masculine identity.

THE PATHWAY TO THE OEDIPAL PHASE

Mahler (Mahler et al., 1975) has emphasized that the period of the rapprochement crisis is more troubled for the girl than for the boy. As we have stated, we believe it is the recognition of the sexual difference that accounts for the divergence in the quality of the rapprochement crisis. In girls, as we have already described, the heightening of the aggressive aspect of the ambivalence to the mother as a result of the recognition of the genital anatomical difference leads to a loosening of the tie to the mother and an increasingly erotic turn to the father, a developmental precondition for the future positive oedipal constellation. In those girls with severe castration reactions, the hostile ambivalence to the mother becomes very intense, the maternal attachment is heightened, and the turn to the father does not occur.

We here present a typical boy's progression through the early genital phase and his emerging sense of sexual identity. We were fortunate in being able to follow this boy through most of his third year, and could identify the early oedipal configuration as it began to emerge.

Jeff, the only child of a mother who was well attuned to him and a father who left the major caretaking responsibilities to his wife during Jeff's first year, discovered his penis at seven and a half months. By 12 months, the landmarks of his separation-individuation progress were well within average range: He was now interested in his own mirror image, objected to having his mother leave him, began to anticipate his father's return home each evening, and was just beginning to walk without assistance. His achievements in symbolic development were age-appropriate in that he had a repertoire of several gestures, including pointing and "bye-bye," and he had a three-word vocabulary.

At about 14 months, Jeff showed behavioral evidence of beginning anal-phase organization. He became interested in toilets and garbage pails, pulled at his soiled diaper selectively, smeared his food, became much more demanding, and flared up in temper tantrums. At about the same time, evidence of urinary organization appeared. He took pleasure in stopping and starting his own urinary stream and became fascinated with his father's urinary stream for the first time, a urinary interest which soon extended to his mother as well.

With this upsurge in urinary interest and awareness, a type of behavior involving the genital area made its first appearance. At 15 months, Jeff began to regularly and rather frequently point at, look at, and pull at his penis, playing a hide-and-seek visual game with it by pulling in and then relaxing his somewhat protuberant abdomen. This new level of genital cathexis was accompanied by a parallel development in that he began to imitate many of his father's activities for the first time: He tried to walk in his father's shoes, draped himself in his father's ties and belts, and initiated a number of games which he now played only with his father.

During the next two months — between his 15th

and 17th months — Jeff's genital play took on a distinctly masturbatory character in that genital self-stimulation was now frequent, more definitely pleasurable, and often culminated in an erection. At 17½ months, he rubbed his penis during each diapering, giggling as he did so, and seemed to invite his mother to share in this pleasure and excitement by glancing up at her with a smile. That there was an element of doing to himself what had previously been done to him was evident from the careful and tender way in which he powdered his own penis on several occasions. With the intensification of his masturbation came several episodes of prolonged and intent inspection of his father's penis as he observed his father's urination. His parents thought that Jeff had now become aware of the father's penis itself, in contrast to his previous interest in the father's urinary process.

The two-month period of intense masturbation began to decline by about 18 months. Jeff now became interested in his own umbilicus as well as those of others about him, and he and his mother developed a mutual umbilical tickling play. The balance of interest in his parents also began to shift at about this time in that he now preferred to kiss his father, whom he eagerly awaited each evening; his general behavior was different over the weekend when his father was home. He continued to show a very active interest in his father's urination.

We consider it likely that the relative inhibition of masturbation which occurred in this boy and his turn to his father for the support of his growing sense of masculine identity were in reaction to Jeff's initial acknowledgment of the sexual anatomical difference. The emergence of his defensive denial was reflected in his avoidance of further confrontation with his mother's genitals, for he would immediately become interested in various objects in the bathroom whenever he accompanied his mother there. We believe that his anxiety over the genital difference was further allayed by displacement to the umbilicus. Yet the strain of the persistent underlying anxiety made itself evident and was reflected in such "body games" as pulling his sleeves down to cover his hands, having his mother question him as to where his hands had gone, and then revealing his hands to her once more with a squeal of delight and a sense of relief. His castration anxiety also seemed to be expressed in Jeff's new preoccupation with keys, pens, and tall trees, all of which shared the attribute of their phallic shape.

Masturbatory activities were resumed at 19¼ months, after an interlude of about five weeks. Several new features had now been added to the former genital behavior: the self-stimulation was more vigorous, with slapping of genitals and thighs, although at times he fingered his penis gently; tumescence was more apt to follow this gentler type of stimulation. Jeff's delight in his own body prompted his parents to institute a "naked time" each evening, when he would dash about the house naked, often stopping rather abruptly to look down at his penis with obvious satisfaction and delight. Anal interest also returned at this time, and Jeff began to use the name he had been given for both stool and penis.[1] Appar-

---

[1] It is of interest that most of the girls had not been given specific names for their genital area during the second year, in contrast to most of the boys, whose mothers usually had a specific name, and often a pet name as well,

ently, both aspects of his body had achieved a new level of more stable mental representation after the brief period of denial. Along with this increased zonal cathexis, Jeff became even more involved with his father. Their play was intense rough-and-tumble, only occasionally interrupted by a brief dash to hide behind his mother's legs. He also began to be interested in certain aspects of the inanimate world in a new way in that he became an avid rock collector.

Such a period of developmental advance on all fronts during which the infant utilizes a variety of defense mechanisms is typical of the means by which anxiety is mastered at this early age. Jeff's sense of his growing masculine identity through his ever-increasing identification with his father was aided by his increasing capacity for symbolization. The interest in rock collecting seemed to be yet another means of mastering his anxiety over the combination of anal and phallic loss.

During the next month and a half, that is, from age 20 to 21½ months, there was some decline in Jeff's masturbatory activity but a burgeoning of phallic-derivative behavior of many types. His relationship with his mother remained loving and tender, but without much erotic quality in it. Jeff shared many new games with his father, most of which involved large-muscle activities. His father would carry Jeff on his shoulders as if they were horse and rider, and Jeff would imitate this game in his father's absence, taking the horse's role himself.

---

for the penis. Here we enter the realm of the cultural as well as parental influence on this area of sexual identity — one where we can merely affirm its importance without supplying actual data concerning unconscious influences which are undoubtedly brought to bear.

He asked after his father during the day, and they often spoke to each other on the telephone. He tended to obey his father's instructions far more diligently than his mother's, despite the fact that his father was by no means a strict disciplinarian. It was particularly touching to see this small boy lean back in his chair, count on his fingers as his father did, and mimic his father's facial expressions and body mannerisms as he gradually seemed to be turning into a small edition of the man he now looked up to so admiringly. This identification extended into the cognitive realm as well: Jeff was able to learn words from his father which his mother had been unable to teach him, and father and son played many word games together. He also began to tinker with the stereo musical equipment, one of his father's favorite pastimes. He was entirely comfortable with his father now, whether his mother was present or not.

Jeff showed a tendency to urinate more frequently when his father diapered him than when his mother did, and at 20¼ months he urinated in a standing posture for the first time. He was clearly excited and proud of this achievement. A brief but intense flurry of preoccupation with knees and elbows emerged a short time later, a seeming displacement from the phallic area itself. Although he followed his mother into the bathroom a few times, once there, he ignored her and instead teasingly snatched some bathroom article and darted out of the bathroom laughing, waiting for his mother to come after him to retrieve the stolen object. This new form of lost-and-found game was one of many to develop during the latter months of Jeff's second year and would seem to be yet another means of coping with his preoedipal castration anxiety, which occasionally broke through. He continued to refuse to have a bowel movement on the toilet, a problem which seemed to reflect the formation of the stool-phallus equation and his continuing struggle with the underlying combined anal and castration anxiety.

On the other hand, Jeff's whole body seemed to assume a phallic connotation for him. He played a "flying" game with his father in which he would run across the room, head ducked forward, arms thrust behind him, while he loudly imitated the "brmm" noise of an airplane. Reaching his father's outspread arms, he would be tossed into the air to the intense excited enjoyment of both father and son. Only occasional disharmony occurred during this rather idyllic period: When the parents kissed or were affectionate with one another, Jeff would intrude himself between them and demand to be kissed by each in turn. He seemed to want to be the center of attraction for both parents rather than wishing either of them for himself alone.

Jeff's interest in his penis slowly began to re-emerge at 21½ months of age. He playfully placed a bottle over it during his bath, and he often leaned forward now to catch a glimpse of it as he sat on the toilet. At 22 months, he urinated into the toilet for the first time and was still fascinated to observe his father's urination. Phallic play continued to be very evident as he straddled and rolled all sorts of vehicles. This progressive trend in the phallic area coincided with Jeff's relinquishment of his earlier oral gratification, his bottle. That this loss was not altogether without its threat for him was reflected in the fact that his old attachments to his blanket and pillow (transitional objects) were now supplemented by several additional attachments to two teddy bears and several other soft stuffed animals which he took to bed each night after they had been kissed ritualistically by both parents at Jeff's insistence.

When Jeff was three years old, we learned, he had grown quite casual about seeing his parents undressed on occasion and paid little if any attention to their genitals. However, when a young uncle visited with the family during Jeff's 28th month, Jeff happened to enter the bathroom while his uncle was bathing. According to his uncle's account of the event, Jeff looked extremely startled and stared at his uncle's penis "as if he were seeing a penis for the first time." Jeff questioned his mother about his uncle's penis for several days thereafter. A week later, Jeff was bathed with one of his girl playmates, an event which had not occurred for some months. Again Jeff appeared to be quite startled. He asked where the girl's penis was and whether his mother had a penis herself and if his own penis could be flushed down the toilet. For the next few days he questioned his mother persistently about whether all the people he knew did or did not possess a penis. This type of waxing and waning of the recognition of the sexual difference is a phenomenon we have noted in many of the other boys in our sample. It seems that the fact of the genital difference as a generalization that applies to all males and females becomes established only gradually over time, particularly in view of the tendency in the boy to deny the genital difference and the possible interference of the denial with cognitive development. It is also possible that such episodes may represent precursors of oedipal development, when a temporary upsurge of erotic feelings toward the mother and rivalry toward the father may threaten the boy's previous denial and identification with the father, the defensive measure whereby the boy was able to maintain the bond with both parents through the vicissitudes of the early genital phase.

When Jeff was 32 months old, he was now regularly standing to urinate into the toilet. However, he would not yet defecate into the toilet, although he was willing to sit as if to defecate. He now played with his penis as he sat, and tumescence often followed this genital handling. On several occasions Jeff had stated that his penis was little and that daddy's was big, and that "the machine would make mine as big as daddy's," foreshadowing the oedipal rivalry about to erupt. When he informed his mother that she did not have a penis and she replied that she had a vagina instead, Jeff responded with, "Vagina hurt," a statement upon which he insisted despite his mother's repeated explanations to the contrary. On the several occasions when he saw his female playmates undressed, however, he would invariably comment upon their lack of a penis in rather matter-of-fact tones.

Aside from the comparisons Jeff made between the size of his own and his father's penis, and the idea that his penis would magically enlarge, there was no clearcut indication that oedipal-phase organization had yet emerged.

It should be noted here that as early as Jeff's first year his mother had decided that he was never to be allowed into the bathroom with her when she was menstruating. Presumably, then, Jeff had arrived at the conclusion that his mother's vagina was "hurt" without his ever having witnessed her menstrual bleeding. Most of the mothers in our group behaved in a similar fashion with regard to protecting their infants from viewing evidence of their menstrual bleeding. It may be that mothers have an unconscious awareness of the centrality of the castration issue for their children, in addition to their conscious educationally invoked ideas about child rearing.

CONCLUSION

In our view then, Freud's original position that sexual-drive organization exerts a special and exemplary role in development remains a valid one, although drive organization is in turn considerably and extensively influenced by events in the sphere of object relations. Very early genital-zone experiences during the first 16 months of life contribute to a vague sense of genital awareness and undoubtedly exert an influence over many ego functions. Some genital sensations probably occur consistently in conjunction with feeding and the other interactions between the mother and her young infant.

With ongoing separation and individuation the genital zone emerges as a distinct and differentiated source of endogenous pleasure somewhere between 15 and 19 months of age, exerting a new and crucial influence upon the sense of sexual identity, object relations, basic mood, and other aspects of ego functioning. This era constitutes an early genital phase, preceding that of the oedipal period: the later oedipal constellation will inevitably be shaped by the preoedipal developments we have described.

We do not consider the discovery of the sexual difference and the new genital sensations of the early genital phase as merely several of many variables that influence the growing sense of identity. They are unique, exemplary, and of equal importance to the oral and anal aspects of psychosexual development which have preceded them. The emergence of the early genital phase, including the preoedipal castration reaction, reactivates and becomes fused with earlier fears of both object and anal loss, and is therefore particularly threatening to the child's still unstable sense of self and object.

We believe that Freud's original position regarding women was correct in so far as his premise that penis envy and the feminine castration complex exert crucial influences upon feminine development. However, these occur earlier than he had anticipated. They are closely intertwined with fears of object and anal loss, and they shape an already developing although vague sense of femininity stemming from early body and affective experiences with both parents. Furthermore, the castration reactions vary in intensity from child to child to a marked degree, and they profoundly influence drive and ego development in both enhancing and inhibiting directions, depending upon specific individual factors. In the boys, the denial of the anatomical difference, supported by the growing identification with the father, is essential to the primary sense of maleness. Where these two trends are interfered with, the basic sense of male sexual identity will remain unstable. We have presented material to illustrate that it is from this period on, from the time of recognition of the genital difference and the infant's reaction to it, that there is a marked divergence between boys and girls in many sectors of their psychological development.

REFERENCES

Abelin, E. L. (1971), Role of the Father in Separation-Individuation. In: *Separation-Individuation*, ed. J. B. McDevitt and C. F. Settlage. New York: International Universities Press, pp. 229–252.

Abraham, K. (1910), Remarks on the Psycho-Analysis of a Case of Foot and Corset Fetishism. In: *Selected Papers on Psychoanalysis.* New York: Brunner Mazel, 1979, pp. 125–136.

_____ (1911), On the Determining Power of Names. In: *Clinical Papers and Essays on Psychoanalysis.* New York: Basic Books, 1955, pp. 31–32.

_____ (1920), Manifestations of the Female Castration Complex. In: *Selected Papers on Psychoanalysis.* New York: Brunner Mazel, 1979, pp. 338–369.

Bak, R. C. (1953), Fetishism. *Journal of the American Psychoanalytic Association*, 1:285–298.

_____ (1968), The Phallic Woman: The Ubiquitous Fantasy in Perversions. *The Psychoanalytic Study of the Child*, 23:15–36. New York: International Universities Press.

Bell, A. (1961), Some Observations on the Role of the Scrotal Sac and Testicles. *Journal of the American Psychoanalytic Association*, 9:261–286.

Brierley, M. (1936), Specific Determinants in Feminine Development. *International Journal of Psycho-Analysis*, 17:163–180.

Bruner, J. S. (1974), The Ontogenesis of Speech Acts. *Journal of Child Language*, 1:1–9.

_____ (1977), Early Social Interaction and Language Acquisition. In:

Studies in Mother-Infant Interaction, ed. H. R. Schaffer. New York: Academic Press, pp. 271–289.

Brunswick, R. M. (1940), The Preoedipal Phase of Libido Development. *Psychoanalytic Quarterly*, 9:293–319.

Casuso, G. (1957), Anxiety Related to the "Discovery" of the Penis. *The Psychoanalytic Study of the Child*, 12:169–174. New York: International Universities Press.

Emde, R. N., Gaensbauer, T. J., & Harmon, R. J. (1976), *Emotional Expression in Infancy: A Biobehavioral Study. Psychological Issues*, Monograph 37. New York: International Universities Press.

Erikson, E. H. (1950), *Childhood and Society*. New York: Norton.

Ferenczi, S. (1913), On Eye Symbolism. In: *Contributions to Psychoanalysis*. New York: Basic Books, 1950, pp. 270–276.

Fliegel, Z. O. (1973), Feminine Psychosexual Development in Freudian Theory. *Psychoanalytic Quarterly*, 42:385–409.

Fraiberg, S. (1972), Some Characteristics of Genital Arousal and Discharge in Latency Girls. *The Psychoanalytic Study of the Child*, 27: 439–475. New York: Quadrangle Books.

Fraser, A. C., ed. (1871), *Bishop George Berkeley*. London: Clarendon Press.

Freud, A. (1951), Observations on Child Development. *Writings*, 4:143–162. New York: International Universities Press, 1968.

―――― (1965), *Normality and Pathology in Childhood. Writings*, 6. New York: International Universities Press.

―――― & Burlingham, D. (1944), *Infants Without Families. Writings*, 3:626–630. New York: International Universities Press, 1973.

Freud, S. (1900), The Interpretation of Dreams. *Standard Edition*, 4 & 5. London: Hogarth Press, 1953.

―――― (1905), Three Essays on the Theory of Sexuality. *Standard Edition*, 7:125–143. London: Hogarth Press, 1953.

―――― (1911), Psycho-analytic Notes on an Autobiographical Account of a Case of Paranoia (Dementia Paranoides). *Standard Edition*, 12: 3–82. London: Hogarth Press, 1958.

―――― (1917), Mourning and Melancholia. *Standard Edition*, 14:239–258. London: Hogarth Press, 1957.

―――― (1920), Beyond the Pleasure Principle. *Standard Edition*, 18: 3–64. London: Hogarth Press, 1955.

―――― (1921), Group Psychology and the Analysis of the Ego. *Standard Edition*, 18:67–143. London: Hogarth Press, 1955.

―――― (1923a), The Ego and the Id. *Standard Edition*, 19:3–66. London: Hogarth Press, 1961.

―――― (1923b), The Infantile Genital Organization of the Libido. *Standard Edition*, 19:141–153. London: Hogarth Press, 1961.

―――― (1925), Some Psychical Consequences of the Anatomical Distinction Between the Sexes. *Standard Edition*, 19:243–258. London: Hogarth Press, 1961.

_____ (1926), Inhibitions, Symptoms and Anxiety. *Standard Edition*, 20:77–174. London: Hogarth Press, 1959.

_____ (1927), Fetishism. *Standard Edition*, 21:149–157. London: Hogarth Press, 1961.

_____ (1931), Female Sexuality. *Standard Edition*, 21:223–243. London: Hogarth Press, 1961.

_____ (1933), New Introductory Lectures on Psycho-Analysis. Lecture 33, Femininity. *Standard Edition*, 22:112–135. London: Hogarth Press, 1964.

_____ (1937), Analysis Terminable and Interminable. *Standard Edition*, 23:211–253. London: Hogarth Press, 1964.

_____ (1938), Splitting of the Ego in the Process of Defence. *Standard Edition*, 23:271–278. London: Hogarth Press, 1964.

Furer, M. (1964), The Development of a Preschool Symbiotic Psychotic Boy. *The Psychoanalytic Study of the Child*, 19:448–469. New York: International Universities Press.

Gillespie, W. H. (1952), Notes on the Analysis of Sexual Perversions. *International Journal of Psycho-Analysis*, 33:397–402.

Greenacre, P. (1950), Special Problems of Early Female Sexual Development. In: *Trauma, Growth, and Personality*. New York: International Universities Press, 1952, pp. 237–258.

_____ (1953a), Certain Relationships Between Fetishism and the Faulty Development of the Body Image. In: *Emotional Growth*. New York: International Universities Press, 1971, pp. 9–30.

_____ (1953b), Penis Awe and Its Relation to Penis Envy. In: *Emotional Growth*. New York: International Universities Press, 1971, pp. 31–49.

_____ (1954), Problems of Infantile Neurosis. In: *Emotional Growth*. New York: International Universities Press, 1971, pp. 50–57.

_____ (1955), Further Considerations Regarding Fetishism. In: *Emotional Growth*. New York: International Universities Press, 1971, pp. 58–66.

_____ (1956), Experiences in Awe of Childhood. In: *Emotional Growth*. New York: International Universities Press, 1971, pp. 67–92.

_____ (1958), Early Physical Determinants in the Development of the Sense of Identity. In: *Emotional Growth*. New York: International Universities Press, 1971, pp. 113–127.

_____ (1960), Further Notes on Fetishism. In: *Emotional Growth*. New York: International Universities Press, 1971, pp. 182–198.

_____ (1966), Problems of Overidealization of the Analyst and of Analysis: Their Manifestations in the Transference and Countertransference Relationship. In: *Emotional Growth*. New York: International Universities Press, 1971, pp. 743–761.

_____ (1968), Perversions. In: *Emotional Growth*. New York: International Universities Press, 1971, pp. 300–314.

_____ (1969), The Fetish and the Transitional Object. In: *Emotional*

Growth. New York: International Universities Press, 1971, pp. 315–334.

———— (1970), The Transitional Object and the Fetish. In: *Emotional Growth*. New York: International Universities Press, 1971, pp. 335–352.

Heinicke, C. M. & Westheimer, I. (1965), *Brief Separations*. New York: International Universities Press.

Hoffer, W. (1949), Mouth, Hand and Ego Integration. *The Psychoanalytic Study of the Child*, 3/4: 49–56. New York: International Universities Press.

Horney, K. (1924), On the Genesis of the Castration Complex in Women. In: *Feminine Psychology*, ed. H. Kelman. New York: Norton, 1967, pp. 37–53.

———— (1926), The Flight from Womanhood. In: *Feminine Psychology*, ed. H. Kelman. New York: Norton, 1967, pp. 54–70.

Jones, E. (1916), The Theory of Symbolism. In: *Papers on Psycho-Analysis*. Baltimore: Williams & Wilkins, 1948, pp. 103–124.

———— (1927), The Early Development of Female Sexuality. In: *Papers on Psycho-Analysis*. Baltimore: Williams & Wilkins, 1948, pp. 438–451.

———— (1933), The Phallic Phase. *International Journal of Psycho-Analysis*, 14:1–33.

———— (1935), Early Female Sexuality. In: *Papers on Psycho-Analysis*. Baltimore: Williams & Wilkins, 1948, pp. 485–495.

Kestenberg, J. (1956), Vicissitudes of Female Sexuality. *Journal of the American Psychoanalytic Association*, 4:453–476.

———— (1968), Outside and Inside, Male and Female. *Journal of the American Psychoanalytic Association*, 16:456–520.

Kleeman, J. M. (1965), A Boy Discovers His Penis. *The Psychoanalytic Study of the Child*, 20:239–266. New York: International Universities Press.

———— (1966), Genital Self-Discovery During a Boy's Second Year: A Follow-Up. *The Psychoanalytic Study of the Child*, 21:358–392. New York: International Universities Press.

———— (1967), The Peek-A-Boo Game. *The Psychoanalytic Study of the Child*, 22:239–273. New York: International Universities Press.

———— (1971), The Establishment of Core Gender Identity in Normal Girls. *Archives of Sexual Behavior*, 1:117–129.

———— (1975), Genital Self-Stimulation in Infant and Toddler Girls. In: *Masturbation: From Infancy to Senescence*, ed. I. Marcus & J. Francis. New York: International Universities Press, pp. 77–106.

Klein, M. (1928), Early Stages of the Oedipus Conflict and of Superego Formation. In: *The Psycho-Analysis of Children*. New York: Norton, 1932, pp. 179–209.

Korner, A. F. (1973), Sex Differences in Newborns with Special Reference to Differences in the Organization of Oral Behavior. *Journal of Child Psychology & Psychiatry*, 14:19–29.

Kris, E. (1951), Some Comments and Observations on Early Autoerotic Activities. In: *Selected Papers*. New Haven: Yale University Press, 1975, pp. 89–113.

Langer, S. K. (1942), *Philosophy in a New Key*. Cambridge: Harvard University Press. New York: Basic Books, 1949.

Lerner, H. (1976), Parental Mislabeling of Female Genitals as a Determinant of Penis Envy and Learning Inhibitions in Women. *Journal of the American Psychoanalytic Association*, 25(Suppl.): 269–283.

Lewin, B. D. (1946), Sleep, the Mouth, and the Dream Screen. In: *Selected Writings*, ed. J. A. Arlow. New York: Psychoanalytic Quarterly, Inc., 1973, pp. 87–114.

Lichtenstein, H. (1961), Identity and Sexuality: A Study of Their Interrelationship in Man. *Journal of the American Psychoanalytic Association*, 9:197–260.

Loewenstein, R. M. (1950), Conflict and Autonomous Ego Development During the Phallic Phase. *The Psychoanalytic Study of the Child*, 5:47–52. New York: International Universities Press.

McDevitt, J. (1975), Separation-Individuation and Object Constancy. *Journal of the American Psychoanalytic Association*, 23:713–742.

Mahler, M. S. (1963), Thoughts about Development and Individuation. *The Psychoanalytic Study of the Child*, 18:307–324. New York: International Universities Press.

⸻ (1966), Notes on the Development of Basic Moods: The Depressive Affect. In: *Psychoanalysis—A General Psychology*, ed. R. M. Loewenstein, L. Newman, M. Schur, & A. J. Solnit. New York: International Universities Press, pp. 156–168.

⸻ (1967), On Human Symbiosis and the Vicissitudes of Individuation. *Journal of the American Psychoanalytic Association*, 15:740–763.

⸻ (1971), A Study of the Separation-Individuation Process and its Possible Application to Borderline Phenomena in the Psychoanalytic Situation. *The Psychoanalytic Study of the Child*, 26:403–424. New York: Quadrangle Books.

⸻ & Furer, M. (1968), *On Human Symbiosis and the Vicissitudes of Individuation. Vol. 1, Infantile Psychosis*. New York: International Universities Press.

⸻ & Gosliner, B. J. (1955), On Symbiotic Child Psychosis. Genetic, Dynamic, and Restitutive Aspects. In: *The Psychoanalytic Study of the Child*, 10:195–212. New York: International Universities Press.

_____, Pine, F., & Bergman, A. (1975), *The Psychological Birth of the Human Infant*. New York: Basic Books.

Money, J. & Ehrhardt, A. A. (1972), *Man and Woman, Boy and Girl*. Baltimore & London: Johns Hopkins University Press.

Moore, B. E. & Fine, B. D., eds. (1968), *A Glossary of Psychoanalytic Terms and Concepts*, second ed. New York: American Psychoanalytic Association.

Müller, J. (1932), A Contribution to the Problem of Libidinal Development of the Genital Phase of Girls. *International Journal of Psycho-Analysis*, 13:361–368.

Murphy, L. (1962), *The Widening World of Childhood*. New York: Basic Books.

Payne, S. M. (1935), A Conception of Femininity. *British Journal of Medical Psychology*, 15:18–33.

Peller, L. E. (1954), Libidinal Phases, Ego Development, and Play. *The Psychoanalytic Study of the Child*, 9:178–198. New York: International Universities Press.

Piaget, J. (1923), *The Language and Thought of the Child*. London: Routledge & Kegan Paul, 1959.

_____ (1936), *The Origins of Intelligence in Children*. New York: International Universities Press, 1952.

_____ (1937), *The Construction of Reality in the Child*. New York: Basic Books, 1954.

_____ (1945), *Play, Dreams and Imitation in Childhood*. New York: Norton, 1951.

Pine, F. & Furer, M. (1963), Studies of the Separation-Individuation Phase. *The Psychoanalytic Study of the Child*, 18:325–342. New York: International Universities Press.

Provence, S. A. & Lipton, R.C. (1962), *Infants in Institutions*. New York: International Universities Press.

Sachs, L. J. (1962), A Case of Castration Anxiety Beginning at Eighteen Months. *Journal of the American Psychoanalytic Association*, 10: 329–337.

_____ (1977), Two Cases of Oedipal Conflict Beginning at 18 Months. *International Journal of Psycho-Analysis*, 58:57–66.

Schur, M. (1955), Comments on the Metapsychology of Somatization. *The Psychoanalytic Study of the Child*, 10:119–164.

_____ (1958), The Ego and the Id in Anxiety. *The Psychoanalytic Study of the Child*, 13:19–220, New York, International Universities Press.

Sperling, M. (1963), Fetishism in Children. *Psychoanalytic Quarterly*, 32:374–392.

Spitz, R. A. (1962), Autoerotism Re-examined. *The Psychoanalytic Study of the Child*, 17:283–315. New York: International Universities Press.

＿＿＿＿ (1965), *The First Year of Life*. New York: International Universities Press.

＿＿＿＿ &Wolf, K. M. (1949), Autoerotism: Some Empirical Findings and Hypotheses on Three of its Manifestations in the First Year of Life. *The Psychoanalytic Study of the Child*, 3/4:85–119. New York: International Universities Press.

＿＿＿＿ (1972), Bedrock of Masculinity and Femininity: Bisexuality. *Archives of General Psychiatry*, 26:207–212.

Stoller, R. J. (1968), *Sex and Gender*. New York: Jason Aronson.

Vigotsky, L. S. (1934), *Thought and Language*. New York: M.I.T. Press, 1962.

Waelder, R. (1932), The Psychoanalytic Theories of Play. In: *Psychoanalysis: Observation, Theory, Application*. New York: International Universities Press, 1976, pp. 84–100.

Werner, H. & Kaplan, B. (1963), *Symbol Formation*. New York: Wiley.

Winnicott, D. W. (1953), Transitional Objects and Transitional Phenomena. A Study of the First Not-Me Possession. In: *Collected Papers*. New York: Basic Books, 1958, pp. 229–242.

＿＿＿＿ (1969), The Use of the Object. *International Journal of Psycho-Analysis*, 50:711–716.

Wulff, M. (1946), Fetishism and Object Choice in Early Childhood. *Psychoanalytic Quarterly*, 15:450–471.

Zilboorg, G. (1944), Masculine and Feminine. *Psychiatry*, 7:257–296.

INDEX